I0762874

BRANT HANSEN

PLUS
20 HAND-DRAWN
ARTISANAL
STICK PEOPLE
PICS

LIVING

THE JOY OF SIMPLE PEACE IN AN ANGRY, ANXIOUS WORLD

Living Unoffended: The Joy of Simple Peace in An Angry, Anxious World

Portions of this book adapted from *Unoffendable* (ISBN: 9781400333592), *Life Is Hard, God Is Good, Let's Dance* (ISBN: 9781400334056), and *Blessed Are the Misfits* (ISBN: 9780718096311).

Published in Nashville, Tennessee, by W Publishing, an imprint of Thomas Nelson. Thomas Nelson titles may be purchased in bulk for educational, business, fund-raising, or sales promotional use. For information, please email SpecialMarkets@ThomasNelson.com.

ISBN 9781400357048 (audiobook)
ISBN 9781400357031 (eBook)
ISBN 9781400357024 (softcover)

Library of Congress Cataloging-in-Publication Data

Printed in the United States of America

CIP data is available upon request

26 27 28 29 30 LBC 5 4 3 2 1

INTRODUCTION

We need to keep talking about this stuff. Even more than before.

That is what my publisher told me when they hit me with the idea for this book. Our culture is, indeed, in the throes of epidemics of both anger and anxiety. And for us to live a different way, we need more reminders, more encouragement than ever. That's what I've been offering in my books for a while now.

My publisher's idea made sense to me. And that's why I went to bat for you, dear reader, to make sure this was the best book possible. I demanded Bonus Features.

These are the Bonus Features that I, Brant Hansen, Insisted Upon:

1. Short "chapters." This isn't because I don't respect your attention span. It's because I respect your time. If a helpful point can be made in four hundred words, why use forty thousand?
2. The inclusion of custom, hand-drawn, artisanal drawings to illustrate my points. These drawings will feature highly abstracted anthropomorphic delineations rendered in a bespoke, minimalist, authentic aesthetic.
3. By that I mean my publisher had to let me draw stick people. True, this feature is mostly for me. But still.

4. Lots of new stuff, in addition to "best of" bits from previous books. All of it to give you a breath of what I hope is fresh air.

5. I insisted we include references to *The Lord of the Rings*, which is a given, but also Taco Bell, G.K. Chesterton, the town of Brainerd, Minnesota, and—obviously—Groupons.

And I wanted it all in one attractive package, which you're holding in your hands right now. I also insisted that the book cover feature a 3-D, holographic sticker of my face. By the time you're reading this, you'll know whether I won this battle. I've been reading this book about negotiating strategies, and there's NO WAY they can stand up to that.

All this to say, this is going to be fun. And hopefully so much more than that. I hope this book adds value to your life, by reminding you of the beauty of practicing the way of Jesus. We humans really are "forgetting machines." We need reminders and encouragers along the way. I hope to be that for you.

And like the good publisher-folks said: We need to keep talking about this stuff.

The way of Jesus is so much better.

Choosing to Be Unoffendable

Okay. So this may sound like the dumbest thing you've ever read, but here goes:

You can choose to be "unoffendable."

I actually heard a guy say this at a business meeting. That is striking to me for a few reasons: (1) I'd never, ever thought about that before; (2) I remember something from a business meeting; and (3) I was actually invited to a business meeting.

I remember the guy saying it's a choice we can make, to just choose not to be offended.

Sure. Right, man. Choose to be unoffendable. Just—you know—choose, as if it's really just up to us.

I found this offensive.

By the way, I just looked up the definition of *offended*, and all the dictionaries say something about anger and resentment. When I'm writing about the word here, then, that's what I mean.

There's another definition, about having your senses affronted, or offended, but that's not the definition we're dealing with here. We just made some homemade barbecue sauce the other day, and we unanimously and immediately agreed, right then and there, that it was highly offensive. That happens.

It's the *taking* of offense, and the very presumption that I'm somehow *entitled* to be angry with someone, that I'm talking about. Surely there's got to be a place for "righteous anger" against someone, right? Surely there are times we are justified in our anger . . .

But what that guy said at the business meeting did get me thinking, because he was so obviously wrong. And besides, since I call myself a Christian person, wasn't I *supposed* to be angry at people for certain things? Isn't being offended *part* of being a Christian?

So I did what any rational, fair-minded, spiritually mature person would do: I scoured the Bible for verses I could pull out to destroy his argument, logically pummel him into submission, and—you know—win.

Problem: I now think he's right. Not only *can* we choose to be unoffendable; we *should* choose that.

We should forfeit our right to be offended. That means forfeiting our right to hold on to *anger*. When we do this, we'll be making a sacrifice that's very pleasing to God. It strikes at our very pride. It forces us not only to think about humility, but to actually be humble.

I used to think it was incumbent upon a Christian to take offense. I now think we should be the most refreshingly unoffendable people on a planet that seems to spin on an axis of offense.

Forfeiting our right to anger makes us deny ourselves, and makes us others-centered. When we start living this way, it changes everything.

Actually, it's not even "forfeiting" a right, because the right doesn't exist. We're told to forgive, and that means anger has to go, whether we've decided our own anger is "righteous" or not.

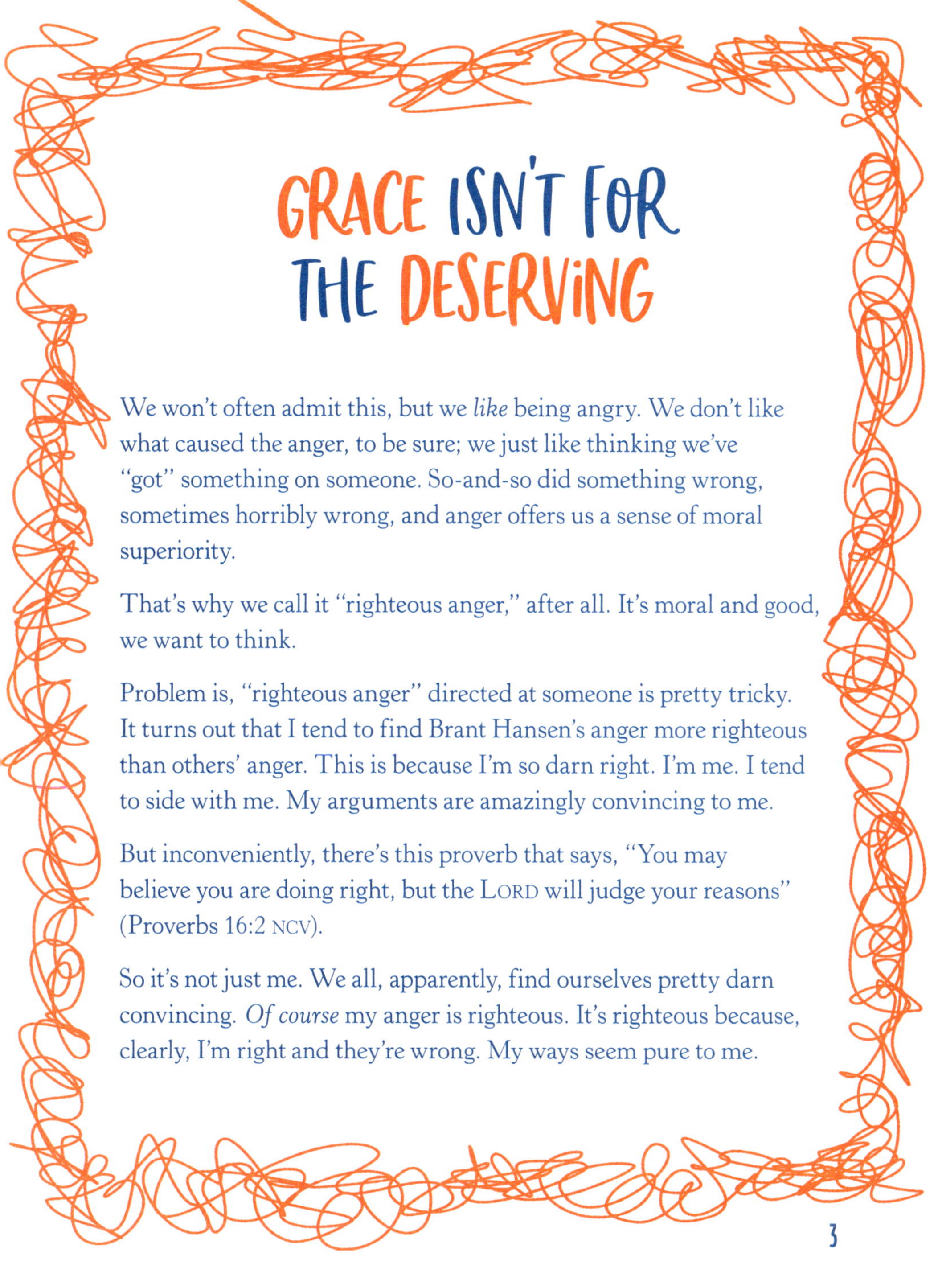

GRACE ISN'T FOR THE DESERVING

We won't often admit this, but we *like* being angry. We don't like what caused the anger, to be sure; we just like thinking we've "got" something on someone. So-and-so did something wrong, sometimes horribly wrong, and anger offers us a sense of moral superiority.

That's why we call it "righteous anger," after all. It's moral and good, we want to think.

Problem is, "righteous anger" directed at someone is pretty tricky. It turns out that I tend to find Brant Hansen's anger more righteous than others' anger. This is because I'm so darn right. I'm me. I tend to side with me. My arguments are amazingly convincing to me.

But inconveniently, there's this proverb that says, "You may believe you are doing right, but the LORD will judge your reasons" (Proverbs 16:2 NCV).

So it's not just me. We all, apparently, find ourselves pretty darn convincing. *Of course* my anger is righteous. It's righteous because, clearly, I'm right and they're wrong. My ways seem pure to me.

Always.

In the moment, everyone's anger *always* seems righteous. Anger is a feeling, after all, and it sweeps over us and tells us we're being denied something we should have. It provides its own justification.

But an emotion is just an emotion. It's not critical thinking. Anger doesn't pause. We have to stop, and we have to question it.

We humans are experts at casting ourselves as victims and rewriting narratives that put us in the center of injustices. And we can repaint our anger or hatred of someone—say, anyone who threatens us—into a righteous-looking work of art. And yet, remarkably, in Jesus' teaching, there is no allowance for "Okay, well, if someone really is a jerk, then yeah—you need to be offended." We're flat-out told to *forgive*, even—especially!—the very stuff that's understandably maddening and legitimately offensive.

That's the whole point: *The thing that you think makes your anger "righteous" is the very thing you are called to forgive.* Grace isn't for the deserving. Forgiving means surrendering your claim to resentment and letting go of anger.

Anger is extraordinarily easy. It's our default setting.

Love is very difficult. Love is a miracle.

OPTING OUT OF POP RELIGION

Lately I've been reading a lot of manifestos by people, usually religious celebrities, who are publicly announcing they're leaving the faith or on their way out the door. They've deconstructed and found they have nothing left.

I do understand where they are coming from. I've seen toxic religion so up close and personal it hurts. As I mentioned, I get this a lot from people who know how I grew up, in a pastor's home filled with terrifying religious hypocrisy: "How in the world did you wind up a Jesus follower?"

It's a fine question.

I've seen such deep ugliness, and not just as a kid. I've seen how professional Christians have transformed so much of "church" into an industry. I've seen people drag Jesus into their political power plays, on the Left and Right. Working in Christian music radio, I've had to protest plans to mislead listeners for fundraising purposes, and I've even quit jobs over it.

I counted the other day—full-time church pastors I've personally known who have cheated on their wives and been found out: fourteen so far, including my dad.

In several incidents, I've been treated dismissively by religious leaders and preachers . . . until they find out I have a platform, which is when I'm suddenly richly deserving of their time and attention.

Ugh.

I've had to do more than a little deconstruction myself, reconsidering what Jesus had in mind for His church and determining what being His disciple means and what it doesn't. I've asked questions about my own motives. Sometimes I've felt like I'm barely hanging on.

But I'm not writing a manifesto or a declaration. (If I did, I would use a quill because quills are cool.) But my point is, I'm not going to write one, because here's something I've noticed about these "I'm leaving Christianity" statements, something very, very odd:

THEY DON'T MENTION JESUS. OR HIS KINGDOM.

You see, this King, and this kingdom, are the reasons I can't leave. So I'm always left wondering, *Okay, I get the critique. Makes sense. But . . . what about Jesus? Isn't that what you were here for? And you don't even mention Him?*

Honestly, if Jesus were just a side issue, I could understand why you'd leave Christianity. I'm not in this for the Christian pop culture or even the T-shirts, including the "Lord's Gym" one where Jesus is doing push-ups with the cross on His back and it says, "Bench Press This!" Not even that one. I'm not in it for that. That's not enough.

I'm not in it for the Christian movies, either, including the one with the guy from *Growing Pains* who works as a fireman, although I bet it was probably a good movie. Maybe. I don't know. My point is, I'm not in this for that.

There's rarely a day on social media when I don't read about some Christian leader doing something scandalous, stupid, or just plain embarrassing. Then I'll see equally embarrassing comments and posts in response from people I know. I feel like I can spend a good portion of the day face-palming. I, like many before me, ask myself whether I seriously want to be associated with this lunacy. What in the world?

The cultural tide is strong, it's pulling the other way, and if my experience of the Christian thing was based on weekly worship concerts with fog machines or church-camp memories or the mega-scandal of the day or politely served chicken sandwiches—however zesty—well, I'm out of here too.

But I'm convinced of this: Once we've seen the reality of the kingdom of God, it's very hard to walk away. It's just too good. Even people like me, people who are cynical by nature or struggle to be spiritual in some emotional way—once we get it, nothing else will do.

There's a lot of religious baggage and immature thinking that can and should be "left behind." And when people tell me, "Don't criticize the church; Jesus would never criticize the church," I get confused because there's Jesus in Revelation 2 taking churches to the woodshed. I've opted out of a lot of pop religion. What I won't do is walk away from this kingdom. No way.

Who Better Than Jesus?

Jesus talked about a pearl merchant, a man who really knew his business, who recognized what was truly valuable. And then he found it! A pearl worth everything he had. So he made his move. He had to have it. He sold everything to get it.

In another parable, Jesus said the kingdom is like a treasure hidden in a field. A guy found the treasure, then hid it again. Why?

So he could go sell everything and buy that field. He had to get the treasure.

The pearl merchant, the treasure-field guy—they were not fools. Quite the opposite.

The kingdom is just too appealing, too poetic, too stunning. The alternatives grow dingy in its light. If you know what's life-and-death valuable, well, you just *have* to have it.

It's always kind of baffled me when Jesus talked about the kingdom in Matthew and said "violent people" raid it. My understanding now is that He was referring to an eagerness to have it; some people will seize it. I've also heard it compared to the eagerness cows have to be let into a fresh, new green pasture after a long winter.[1]

So yes, I can talk about the abuses and weirdness of religion and things done in the name of Jesus. But I'm not leaving Jesus or my brothers and sisters who seek Him.

There may be fewer of us in the days ahead, at least in the US, where I live. But I feel now I've become like Jesus' friends, the ones who stayed after everyone else walked away from Him. Jesus turned to them and asked, "You do not want to leave too, do you?" (John 6:67).

Nope.

Where else do I go? No one else has the words of life.

And no one else offers this joy, this peace, this sense of well-being regardless of circumstances. No one. The alternatives, I'm convinced, don't work.

I can't leave, because now I've seen too much, including a lot of things I'm going to tell you about in this book. I'm not going anywhere. Yes, there are religious hypocrites in the world. But I'm not going to give them the power to stop me from the best relationship of my life.

This gospel, this good news that the kingdom is now available to all of us? It's too good to trade in for a sweet rush of very temporary freedom. Jesus makes too much sense. I have to trust someone—we all do—so really: Who better than Jesus?

I FEEL LIKE UNFROZEN CAVEMAN LAWYER

I just watched part of a big church worship service online. There was a lot of music and smoke and stuff and then I saw what looked like a—*Is that a roller-coaster track?*

Why yes, it is a roller-coaster track.

The disco song "Roller Coaster of Love" played and there was a theme park backdrop with a roller coaster in the center of the stage. Standing in the midst of this spectacle was a guy wearing a suit. I assumed he was the pastor because he started talking about how life is a roller coaster and so forth. It all sort of tied in.

I saw video thumbnails off to the side on my screen, and, wait—*Is that another church roller coaster?*

Why yes, it is another church roller coaster. This second coaster had more people on it, and another guy with a microphone, and he, too, talked about how life is a roller coaster, and so forth.

The roller-coaster thing was getting to be old hat by now, so I clicked to the next . . . *Does that say, "Super Bowl Sunday Service"? Is that the pastor in a football uniform?*

Why yes, yes, it is.

And is he punting a Bible through some goalposts?

Yes, he appears to be punting a Bible through some goalposts.

I don't always understand a lot of Christian-themed or church-themed stuff. It confuses me. Honestly, I don't see the connection to Jesus. Perhaps I am naïve. I feel like the classic Phil Hartman "Unfrozen Caveman Lawyer" sketch, when he's in court, wearing a suit, explaining:

> "Ladies and gentlemen of the jury. I'm just a caveman. I fell on some ice and later got thawed out by some of your scientists. Your world frightens and confuses me! Sometimes the honking horns of your traffic make me want to get out of my BMW, and run off into the hills, or wherever. My primitive mind can't grasp these concepts."
>
> But there is one thing I *do* know: When a man like my client slips and falls on a sidewalk in front of a public library, then he is entitled to no less than two million in compensatory damages, and two million in punitive damages. Thank you.[2]

So yes, your roller coasters and your punting of Bibles . . . they confuse me. My primitive mind can't grasp these concepts. So much simply does not compute.

Maybe you can relate.

As I pointed out earlier, I'm not going to let religious hypocrites stand in the way of the best relationship of my life. I'm simply not going to give them that power.

Same thing goes for the, uh—how to say, kindly?—"goofiness" that gets a Christian veneer. The consumeristic, individualistic, entertainment-oriented weirdness; the divisions and divisiveness; the power trips and politics and clashing of egos, all of it.

I'm not going to react to that. I can't. And I encourage you not to either.

It's not that these things are unimportant or undeserving of critique or correction. It's just that you don't want this to become *the stuff* of your "spiritual life."

I know the Lord wants to walk with me. I want to partner with Him. My criticism of all the ridiculousness can crowd out Jesus. I've seen it happen to others.

But I've decided I'm not going to let that happen. I can easily clang on for the rest of my life about the offensive ways of cartoonish religious culture, but I'd rather this be the tune and melody of my soul:

> Search me, God, and know my heart;
> test me and know my anxious thoughts.
> See if there is any offensive way in me,
> and lead me in the way everlasting.
>
> (PSALM 139:23–24)

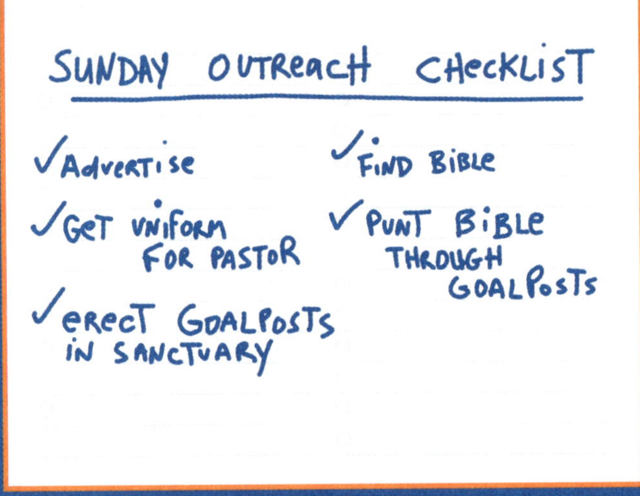

Am I a Fraud?

So much of living life free of anger toward others begins with being thankful for Jesus' patience with us. We're so quick, by nature, to ask hard questions of others. But what about of ourselves?

Every now and then we'll ask listeners on our radio show, "What if you were trapped on an elevator with Jesus? What if you knew it would be a couple of hours before the rescue crew got there? You could talk about anything. What would you ask Him?"

Most people want to ask about pain and suffering and why God allows it. Or they want to know how their grandma's doing. That kind of thing.

Fair enough, but I know what I would want to ask Him. If I could choke out the question, I'd want to ask this:

Am I a fraud?

Please tell me I'm not. Please tell me You're proud of me. Please tell me You know I struggle, but no, I'm not a fraud at all. I'd love to hear it.

I know, in my head, all about grace, and I'm so thankful for it. I think it's beautiful. I know, in my head, that God loves sinners and failures. But I feel like everything I do is tainted with some selfishness. And with my seeming inability to sense God's presence . . . is it possible God could still be proud of me?

Oddly enough, this fraud issue comes to mind, for some, with regard to Teresa of Calcutta, now a Catholic saint, after her correspondence of nearly fifty years was made public.

Here she was, an outspoken follower of Jesus on an international stage, but when it came to warm, religious feelings, she had nothing. And that bothered her deeply. She kept serving the poor, kept praying, kept leading, but she confided in her letters to confessors that she also felt like God had abandoned her.

She wrote that "the silence and emptiness is so great that I look and do not see, listen and do not hear."[3]

Just a few months later she was onstage in Oslo, accepting the Nobel Peace Prize, talking confidently of a Jesus she knew, a Christ who brings joy for all of us. When she started her mission in Calcutta in the 1940s, she was young and excited and felt so close to God. Then, from 1948 until her death in 1997, she was spiritually dry. Yet she continued as an outspoken missionary.

Was she a fake?

Christopher Hitchens certainly thought so. The late, leading atheist and tremendously gifted writer wrote a book accusing Teresa of running from the obvious: Her lack of God-feelings were due to the fact that God didn't exist. He said, "She was no more exempt from the realization that religion is a human fabrication than any other person. . . ."[4]

If she was a fake, I'm not even sure what that makes me. She sacrificed her own comfort to care for the sick and dying.

Me? I get paid to talk between the songs on the radio.

Somehow, the Lord sees through it all, to the very heart of us. He knows us better than we know ourselves . . . and still wants to be with us. Who am I to live a life of offense at others?

THAT GUY IS AN IDIOT

Choosing not to take offense is not about simply ignoring wrongs. If someone, say, cuts in front of you in line, you can address the situation. You don't have to simply accept it. But you can act without contempt, anger, and bitterness.

Yes, there is right and wrong, and what Jesus has done for us is the antidote to both fuzzy-minded relativism and self-righteous religiosity. According to the radical teaching of Jesus, I stand as guilty, morally, as any other sinner, period.

Whatever anyone's done to me, or to anyone else, I stand just as guilty. People have lied to me, but I've lied too. People have been unfaithful to me, but I've been unfaithful too. People have hurt me, and I've hurt them. I get angry toward murderers, and then here comes Jesus, telling me if I've ever *hated* someone—and I have—I am the murderer's moral equal.

No one likes to hear this. We want to think people are worse than us. It's one of our favorite pastimes.

Don't believe me? An experiment: Go to a mall food court, grab a chicken kabob or something, sit down, and listen to the conversations around you. Compare how often people are telling stories about hurtful, wrong things other people did, versus confessing hurtful, wrong things they, themselves, have done.

We're brilliant at this. Geniuses, really. Would that the Nobel Committee had a prize for this.

Happens in traffic all the time. The other day, I was leaving our gym's parking lot, waiting in my car to turn left, sitting toward the middle of the exit, and some guy pulled in quickly and almost hit me. My mental response: *Geez, that guy's an idiot.*

And then, this very morning, I was the one entering the lot, and some guy was sitting there waiting, in the exact same place I'd been, and I thought, *Geez, that guy's an idiot.*

Geez. That guy's an idiot. I've done the *exact* same thing he was doing . . . but *that* guy's an idiot. And the other guy who did *exactly* what I was now doing? Yeah, that guy's an idiot too. "That" guy is always wrong, because he's always that guy. I'm *always* this guy.

In other words: Everybody's an idiot but me. I'm awesome.

Go, me.

(Inspiring quote for you to highlight and post on social media, immediately: "Everybody's an idiot but me. I'm awesome."
—@branthansen)

Moral of the story: The other guy is always the jerk. Many times in my life, I've vocalized, in traffic, something like, "Man, what a jerk." I can't remember ever, not once, saying, "Man, I'm a jerk." Why? Because I'm a victim. My intentions are pure. Other people are the perps. I'm never a perp.

It's as natural as breathing, but that doesn't make it right. It's as universal as eating, but that doesn't make it right either. Because whatever they did? *We're just as guilty.*

I'm not entitled to my anger against them, and I'm not entitled to *think* I'm entitled to my anger. And yet, many tell me that we can, even should, keep our anger for a time. I ask, "How long are you allowed?" and I've heard the same answer, many times: "You can keep it for a little while."

Sounds reasonable. Sure. Absolutely. But merely "reasonable" isn't what we're going for here. We want to follow the gospel, wherever it takes us. God has a way for us to live—a humility that He has called us to—and it's the way we humans happen to really flourish. It's how you will flourish.

THE BIG '90S QUESTION:

EVEN BIGGER THAN "SERIOUSLY, WHY ARE WE WEARING ALL THIS FLANNEL?"

In the '90s, we had things called "compact discs" and we wore lots of flannel and guys "frosted" the tips of their hair. We also, for like a whole year, got really into "Riverdance," which is when you move your legs like crazy but keep your upper body totally still because authentic Irish people hate using their arms.

We also had a fad, and it hasn't completely gone away, because just yesterday I saw a guy wearing a "WWJD?" bracelet.

"What would Jesus do?" is a great question, but it's not a question we want to be asking ourselves all the time. Why? Because we don't want to *need* to.

Sometimes, we don't even have time to ask the question. We have to react right away.

Say a jerky guy cuts in front of you in the Walmart self-checkout area. You calmly say, "Hey, I was next," and he laughs and moves ahead in line. Do you think, *I think I will shove him. Yes, I will shove him, and perhaps I will call him a dirty name.*

But then you look down at your bracelet. *But would Jesus do that? Would He shove this guy? I bet He wouldn't. But what would Jesus do in this situation at Walmart? Perhaps Jesus would ask the guy a question that would penetrate his very soul. Or fashion a cord of whips. Or maybe He would . . .*

By this point, the whole thing is over. The guy is gone.

It sounds goofy, maybe, but most of life is this way. We respond in the moment. So, while "What would Jesus do?" is a helpful question, here's what we want to do: *Become a different kind of person.* The kind of person who would respond as Jesus would.

Responding like Jesus comes from spending time with Jesus. It comes from reading Scripture about Him (and all of Scripture is ultimately about Him, by the way) and growing in our understanding of why He was doing and saying the things He did.

Becoming a person who responds like Jesus would comes from talking to God. It comes from asking for wisdom. It comes from God's Spirit working in and through us. And it comes, like practically anything else worth getting better at, with practice.

I recently learned piano. At first, I couldn't just sit down and play, say, Billy Joel stuff. But now? I can do it, because I became the sort of person who can do it.

We *practice* forgiveness. We *practice* gratitude. These things change us. These things become easier. They become second nature. Thank the Lord, our personality can get a renovation.

Peaceful? Forgiving? Patient? Discerning in the moment? It's just who you are. Sure, you didn't start that way. You became a different person.

BEING OFFENDED IS A TIRING BUSINESS

When I talk about living unoffendable I often hear this objection: "What about being angry at sin, Brant?"

"Of course, we're supposed to be angry at sin."

It's probably worth noting that, usually, when this question is asked of me, it's about something more specific. By "sin," we mean *other people's sin*.

Are we to cling to anger at their sin? God took out His wrath on Jesus for other people's sin. And I believe Jesus suffered enough to pay for it, and my sin too. I'm so thankful for that. He will deal with others' sins; it's not my deal.

That's a huge relief. Again, life is better this way.

As for my own sin, well, He says He's taken that sin away from me as far as the east is from the west (Psalm 103:12). I suppose I could whip up some anger, but I'm honestly just stuck feeling grateful right now.

What's more, for those who still want to make anger a nutritious part of their spiritual breakfasts: In the Bible's "wisdom literature," anger is always—not sometimes, always—associated with foolishness, not wisdom. The writer recognized that, yes, anger may visit us, but when it finds a residence, it's "in the lap of fools" (Ecclesiastes 7:9).

Let that sink in. When anger lives, that's where it lives: in the lap of a fool.

Thinking we're *entitled* to keep anger in our laps—whether toward the sin of a political figure, a news network, your dumb neighbor, your lying spouse, your deceased father, whomever—is perfectly natural, and perfectly foolish.

Make no mistake. Foolishness destroys.

Being offended is a tiring business. Letting things go gives you energy.

A RADICALLY BETTER WAY TO LIVE

Author Frank Viola believes that Christians are more easily offended than anyone else.[5] I think Frank is brilliant, but I actually don't think that's true. In my experience, people—all people—thrive on being offended. It makes us feel more righteous to get aggravated at the behavior of other people. And that's true of all of us, not just religious folk.

Shoot, we get offended by the behavior of people we don't even know. We'll go out of our way to do it, consuming news to hear what outrageous thing some celebrity did or said. Our whole culture does this. Taking offense is a national sport. And as for Viola's claim that Christians are the worst, well, I lived near San Francisco, and while it's largely a post-Christian culture, there are plenty of things one can do or think that the culture there will find terribly offensive.

It's actually a very long list. It's just a different list.

Natural as this is, Jesus came along and gave us a distinctly supernatural, and radically better, way to live. (Oddly, working in Christian media, I hear from a lot of people who are all about living a "radical" Christian life. *Radical* is a great word. But when it comes to something as radical as, say, dropping our right to offense or anger . . . ? No thanks.)

It's true that sometimes people try to offend us, and they're intentionally hurtful and spiteful. And yet, there Jesus is, on the cross, saying, "Father, forgive them. They don't know what they're doing."

A fair question, then: Is that same Jesus, living in and through me, still saying *that*?

LET'S HEAR IT FOR THE BOOK OF PSALMS

"The Psalms," wrote Joni Eareckson Tada, "wrap nouns and verbs around our pain better than any other book."[1]

Wow, is that ever true.

And then there's this about the Psalms from Svetlana Alliluyeva: "Their fervid poetry cleanses one, gives one strength, brings hope in moments of darkness. Makes one look critically into oneself, convict oneself, and wash one's heart clean with one's own tears. It is the ever-burning fire of love, of gratitude, humility, and truth."[2]

Yes, that's so good.

And then there's this quote from me, Brant Hansen: "I hate to say it, maybe, but I kinda like the part where the psalmist wants God to punch people in the face."

My quote isn't as profound, but there it is. Like in Psalm 3:7:

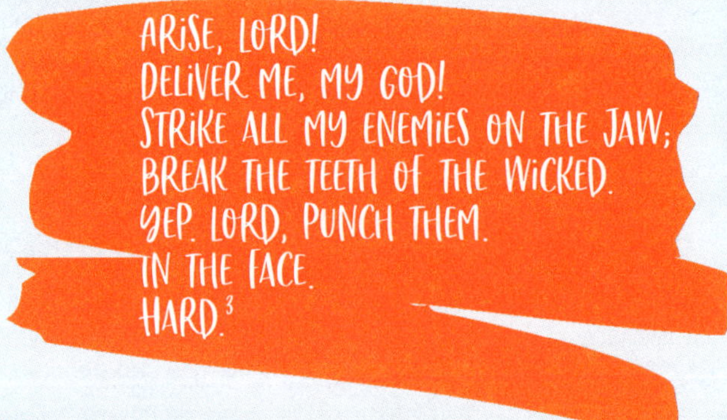

Scan this QR Code to listen to Brant's song, "Break Their Teeth" (inspired by Psalm 3).

Why do I like this, you may ask? I'm the *Unoffendable* guy, right?

Because we're getting a glimpse into a believer's inner life with God. This passage is not prescriptive and it's not saying we should cultivate a desire for vengeance. It's just gut-level honest. Like the psalmist in Psalm 88, who asks, "Why, LORD, do you reject me . . . ?" and concludes with "Darkness is my only friend" (Psalm 88:14, 18).

If you feel angry, talk to God about it. The beauty of praying with this level of honesty is that you're not "venting," which has been shown repeatedly to be ineffective. Venting just works us up all over again.[4] It's like being thirsty and drinking seawater. It seems like it should help, but it makes things worse. As one researcher put it, "Venting anger is like using gasoline to put out a fire."[5]

Why? Because rehearsing the wrongs of others feeds our sense of moral superiority.

When I'm deeply, vulnerably honest with God about my life, I'm in a safe place. This is because He won't let me get away with my own self-righteous delusions. Even as I'm laying out my case, I'm more aware of my dependence on Him and what He's willing to forgive in me.

What's more, God can help me with my anger, at the deepest level. Like a gifted surgeon who can remove a deadly cancer without injuring the patient, God can remove my anger without shaming me.

So yes, I'm thankful for the Psalms. All of them, including the darkest and, you know, the most dentally destructive.

The Lord is our safe place. He wants to change us, and He's the One to do it.

Rethinking Is Hard

A friend of mine once said something I've been thinking about ever since: "Everyone, whether they admit it or not, believes in God. It's just that many don't trust Him." Deep down, they don't think He's truly good or that He could really be *for* them.

I think my friend could be right. I suppose it all comes down to what we think about when we think about God. If you read the stories about Jesus in the Bible, you'll see Him constantly trying to get people to re-think (literally what "repent" means) what they think they know about God and how He works.

Rethinking is hard. Shoot, thinking is hard. But getting people to reconsider stuff? Almost impossible. Maybe that's why Jesus kept saying to crowds, "If just one of you would repent, all of heaven would throw a massive party" (Luke 15:7, my paraphrase).

We don't usually like being told we need to rethink, but there's Jesus, telling us to do it. He's telling us we need to update our imaginations about God. (Notice all the times He said stuff like "You've heard it said . . . ," and then "but I tell you . . .")

Weirdly, people resented it even though Jesus was saying, in so many different ways, "Look, folks: God is better than you think. You can trust Him. Because of Him, you're safe in this world. You can go all in with Him. Even in the worst-case scenario: He's still got you."

Many won't believe it. Rethinking is so hard, we'll often choose anxiety and anger instead.

I saw an article on the tech site Gizmodo called "7 Moments in the Bible When Jesus Acted Very Un-Jesus-Like."[6] From the writer's perspective, it was out of character for Jesus to do the stuff Jesus did. That's like all of us, I guess: We have an idea what God is like, and we're not going to let anyone or anything, including God Himself, get in the way of it.

Lord, we ask You to politely stay in the idiom we have made for You. Amen.

But think about it: What if He's better? What if He has a particular personality, and it's a great one? Honestly: Would I want to get to know Him more, or just stick with my presumptions? What if having the right ideas about who God really is would give us a sense of well-being that could go with us anywhere and through absolutely anything?

I want to keep learning. I know I need to. I hope you see in this book how good God really is, and that you're in a much better place when you realize you can fully trust Him. To learn, we must be humble about what we know, and what we don't.

I love this prayer from Thomas Merton. Maybe you will too:

> My Lord God, I have no idea where I am going. I do not see the road ahead of me. I cannot know for certain where it will end. Nor do I really know myself, and the fact that I think I am following your will does not mean that I am actually doing so. But I believe that the desire to please you does in fact please you. And I hope I have that desire in all that I am doing. I hope that I will never do anything apart from that desire. And I know that if I do this you will lead me by the right road, though I may know nothing about it. Therefore I will trust you always though I may seem to be lost and in the shadow of death. I will not fear, for you are ever with me, and you will never leave me to face my perils alone.[7]

He promises He will hear us when we humbly cry out to Him. I can vouch for that.

you know, that wasn't very Christ-like of you to say that.

But I'm christ.

I know, but still.

NO MATTER WHAT, WE'RE HOPEFUL

A question for you: Based on whatever knowledge you have of Jesus, if you could choose only one word to describe Him, what would you choose?

Dallas Willard, a very wise, extraordinarily learned man whom I often quote, picked a word that still has me thinking. Of all the words at his disposal, he picked this:

Relaxed.[8]

I'm still mulling over that one, but I like it. Jesus really doesn't seem anxious, does He? He's certainly not hurried. He's in the moment. He's not stressing about getting everything done. He's not bothered by deadly storms; we know that—He brings cushions for those.

Relaxed.

So if I believe the things Jesus believes, I will also be relaxed. And you know what? One fun thing about living in a highly anxious, highly hurried society: When you're relaxed, when you don't freak out? It freaks people out.

They don't quite know what to do with it. I think they're drawn to it too. In a world of insecurity, security draws people in. A secure person, whose mind isn't cluttered with hurry and worry, can intently listen.

And listeners are in short supply. We can see that with the overwhelming demand for counseling. If you can focus on someone else, and ask genuinely curious questions, people will wonder what's right with you.

There's this scripture that's been misused (haven't they all?) to smack people over the head with theological arguments. It's where Peter said to "always be prepared to give an answer to everyone," and I've had people tell me that's why I should study stuff—to argue with people and win.

But that misses the entire point of the scripture, because it goes on, and I'll italicize something here:

Always be prepared to give an answer to everyone who asks you to give *the reason for the hope* that you have. (1 Peter 3:15)

It's like Peter even anticipated people getting the wrong impression, because he continued by telling people to "do this with gentleness and respect."

Think about that: Peter expected us to be so different that other people actually notice how hopeful we are, even in the midst of . . . anything and everything. No matter what, we're hopeful. Not complaining. Not griping. Not going on about how the country is going to hell in a handbasket.

In case we want to say, "Yeah, but we are living in special times. Christians are losing their rights, and there's rampant injustice, and . . . ," it's worth reading the whole letter from Peter. The people he was writing to? They were suffering for their faith. He continually referenced this, knowing what they were going through. He was saying yes, people are going to try to hurt you, but don't be afraid. They'll ask why you're so hopeful, so be ready with a gentle answer.

A STRANGE AND AWESOME WAY TO LIVE

Hope isn't the only thing that freaks people out in a wonderful way.

The entire way of life that Jesus gave us is so countercultural, and not just counter to our culture either. I mean, seriously, who *loves* their enemies, for real?

The Sermon on the Mount is profoundly freeing in a thousand ways, but even beyond that, it's also a way of life that leaves people wondering, *Can I really do that? Is that allowed? Can we truly forgive people? Live without fear? Not worry about anything? Not live in anger? Give people more than they ask for? If forced to go one mile, go an extra one? Turn the other cheek if someone hits you in the face?* This is a strange and awesome way to live. I say we try it. So did Brennan Manning:

> If indeed we [Christ followers] lived a life in imitation of his [Jesus], our witness would be irresistible. If we dared to live beyond our self-concern; if we refused to shrink from being vulnerable; if we took nothing but a compassionate attitude toward the world; if we were a counterculture to our nation's lunatic lust for pride of place, power, and possessions; if we preferred to be faithful rather than successful, the walls of indifference to Jesus Christ would crumble. A handful of us could be ignored by society; but hundreds, thousands, millions of such servants would overwhelm the world. Christians filled with the authenticity, commitment, and generosity of Jesus would be the most spectacular sign in the history of the human race. The call of Jesus is revolutionary. If we implemented it, we would change the world in a few months.[9]

We can do this, you know. It's not impossible to learn to follow Jesus. We can love our enemies. We can learn how to forgive people and live without anger. We can learn more and more how to trust God day-to-day. These are doable things, and they are things that make life more joyful. Peace is at hand—the inner kind that everyone is looking for.

IT REALLY ISN'T THAT CONFUSING

I just did an interview on a big Christian radio broadcast. I talked about how we can forgive and pray for our enemies. I told the host that churches could teach more about how to do this.

"Huh, you're right," he said. "I don't think I've ever, in my entire life, heard a sermon about how to do that, how to pray for our enemies."

The man is in his sixties. He's a thoughtful leader, at the epicenter of American evangelicalism, and doesn't remember hearing a sermon about an absolutely central command of Jesus. I appreciated his honesty.

But does that seem like a problem? It seems like a problem to me.

I suspect we'd rather debate theology than actually do the things Jesus told us to do. In fact, some of our theology seems designed to make us think we can ignore Jesus' commands.

But we can do the things Jesus told us to do. Right now, even. Praying for our enemies is a command that's easy to understand. We don't have to be experts to obey. We just have to, you know, quit not obeying.

I imagine this conversation sometimes:

Jesus: I want you to pray for your enemies.

Us: Okay, we will study how to pray for our enemies.

Jesus: I want you to pray for your enemies. Just start.

Us: Okay, we will start a small group that studies the new Christian bestseller, *Great Starts: How to Start Studying Things.*

Jesus: I'm saying you can pray for your enemies right now.

Us: Ah! We get it: You're saying You died on the cross for our sins and now we are truly free.

Jesus: I'm saying that I want you to pray for your actual enemies, right now.

Us: Agreed! Somebody should write a worship song called "Right Now!" It would be a hit.

Jesus: (sighs heavily) (looks to the heavens)

Us: With guitars and stuff.

But you really can do this, starting today. You are equipped. You know what you need to know. You don't need to buy seven more books and debate the concept with your friends.

Unless they are written by me. Please buy those books.

But you get my point—we just have to start.

what is,
"pray"?

what is,
"enemies"?

whaT is,
"foR"?

what is,
"youR"?

wow,
you Guys

ANGER CAN'T LIVE HERE

Your life will become less stressful when you give up your right to anger and offense. And by the way, if you don't, you're doomed. So there's that too.

C. S. Lewis wrote:

> One man may be so placed that his anger sheds the blood of thousands, and another so placed that however angry he gets he will only be laughed at. But the little mark on the soul may be much the same in both. Each has done something to himself which, unless he repents, will make it harder for him to keep out of the rage next time he is tempted, and will make the rage worse when he does fall into it. Each of them, if he seriously turns to God, can have that twist in the central man straightened out again: each is, in the long run, doomed if he will not. The bigness or smallness of the thing, seen from the outside, is not what really matters.[10]

Forgive in the big things and the small things. Don't take offense.

In fact, the stuff that usually might offend us is a huge opportunity! Jesus told us we will be forgiven as we forgive others.

Fact is, most of us don't get that many opportunities to forgive. Once I realized that, traffic went from being an exercise in anger to "forgiveness practice." Life is so much better that way.

I used to be scandalized by others' moral behavior. I'm just not anymore. It frees up a lot of mental space, and we probably need more of that, to pause and reflect on what matters in life. Sure, I've used my free mental space for baseball statistics and Duran Duran lyrics, but I can do better. So can you.

It's not that I think that potentially offensive behavior is "right" or "good." Not even close. It's just that it's not about me. I'm not going to be threatened or scandalized by someone else's immoral behavior.

So what if—just dreaming out loud here—Christians were known as the people you couldn't offend?

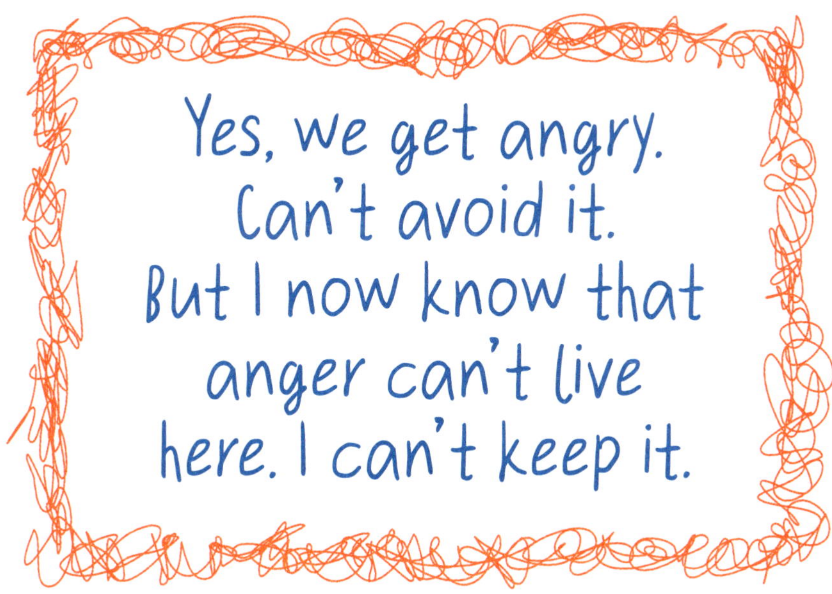

Make Him a Plaque

Offense obscures our vision. Removing offense enables us to see people in wonderful, new ways.

I once worked part-time as a baseball announcer for minor-league teams and, occasionally, during March, for major-league spring-training games. I was the guy they'd call to fill in for a friend of mine named John, who's an absolutely brilliant announcer, and a very well-known radio pro too.

John is a class act. He arrives at each game impeccably dressed, highly organized, and briefcase in hand. That's how he rolls. He's polished. He's polite. He's clean. He's smooth. He's successful. He's also a professing Christian.

Seated next to John at each game is his polar opposite in the behavior department. Bill (I changed the name here) is a grizzled former player whose life has taken some twists and turns for the worse. He's boisterous and foul. His language is remarkably crude. Pornographic, even.

He's very tough to take.

As I worked with Bill, filling in for John, I wondered, *Wow! How does John, who's even more take-charge, blunt, and straitlaced than I am, deal with this guy? And it's night in, night out. I can't imagine how he handles this.*

When profane Bill found out I was friends with buttoned-down John, he gave me my answer. I braced myself. I'll leave the profanity out, but it went something like this:

"You're friends with John, really?"

"Oh, yeah."

"You know what? I got something to say about that guy. That guy, John, is . . ." He paused. Then, momentarily, he continued: "A couple of weeks ago, you know what he did? He brought in a plaque he had made for me. It was the magazine cover from back in the day, me and my teammates. He had an original cover put on the plaque, and he gave it to me to honor me."

Bill was actually tearing up.

"You know what?" he went on. "That guy is really good to me. And he just treats everyone the same up here. All of us the same. The interns, me, the stadium manager, everybody. He just treats us all like he loves us."

Several seconds passed before he finally concluded, "I still can't believe he did that for me."

I emailed John after the game and told him that I'd just heard one of the greatest compliments ever, and it was about him: *He treats us all the same.*

John simply refused to be offended. He was free to love Bill just the way he was.

My instinct, and I'm sure the instincts of many in Bill's life, was to tell Bill to shut up, or at least watch his mouth, or get his act together. Or maybe I could ignore him.

But John? John went and made him a plaque.

GOD SEES THINGS WE DON'T

Choosing "unoffendability" frees us to love people in risky but profound ways.

Jesus is this way with the most morally embarrassing people. You can't find a single story in the Bible where He's so disgusted, so scandalized by someone's moral behavior, that He writes him off. It just doesn't happen.

In fact, a friend recently pointed out something to me that I had never noticed or thought about before. I think it's remarkable.

In John 13, Jesus is having a last meal with His closest friends and followers. He tells them that He will soon have to leave them, and where He's going, they won't be able to follow Him.

Peter objects to this and tells Him that he wants to follow and that he'd even give his life for Jesus.

Then Jesus says, "Will you lay down your life for My sake? Most assuredly, I say to you, the rooster shall not crow till you have denied Me three times" (John 13:38 NKJV).

That's the end of the scene, and it's pretty chilling. The chapter ends right there.

But here's what I'd never thought about: The scene *isn't* actually over. Yes, there's a chapter break, but "chapters" aren't in the original. Bible translators added those centuries later to help us find things in the Bible.

The next chapter, John 14, starts with this:

> Let not your heart be troubled; you believe in God, believe also in Me. In My Father's house are many mansions; if it were not so, I would have told you. I go to prepare a place for you. And if I go and prepare a place for you, I will come again and receive you to Myself; that where I am, there you may be also. (verses 1–3 NKJV)

So think about this: When Peter insists that he is even willing to die for Jesus, Jesus tells him, "No, you'll betray Me. You'll deny Me—three times. *But don't let your heart be troubled. Believe in Me. I'm going to prepare a special place for you—and I'm coming back to get you!*"

Jesus wouldn't even let hypocrisy, betrayal, backstabbing, lying, and abandonment stop Him from loving Peter. He saw something in Peter that Peter could not have possibly seen in himself. And sure enough, in the book of Acts, there's Peter, boldly putting his life on the line to tell people the good news about what God has done for them.

Yes, God sees things we don't. We can risk loving people—incredibly difficult, insulting people—because He loves us.

That person you find so offensive? Somehow, God sees something there. Something you don't. Ask Him what it is. Maybe He'll show you. I bet He wants to.

THE ENDLESS CYCLE

Ever read *The Count of Monte Cristo*? I loved it.

Well, I loved it for the first couple hundred pages. And then it got weird. It's about a guy named Edmond Dantes who's wrongfully imprisoned. Once he escapes, he gets rich and then spends his life systematically destroying the lives of all his enemies. It's one cold, complex, calculated plot after another. It continues for years.

I started off rooting for him, but toward the end of the novel, I found myself thinking, *Bro, enough is enough. You've more than gotten even. Geez.*

But Dantes's revenge tour keeps going and going. It reminded me a bit of Genghis Khan, who was greatly displeased when his envoy was killed by the leaders of the massive Khwarazmian Empire.

What's that? You've never heard of the Khwarazmian Empire? That's because Genghis Khan was, you know, displeased. So he destroyed the whole thing. In the process, he killed more than a million people.

Over-the-top examples, sure, but revenge is just how humans roll. We have a taste for it—even crave it. We love getting even.

But we never do get truly even, do we? The last party to attack does not say, "Fair enough. We're even now." (fist-bump emoji)

No, it's an endless cycle we see repeated throughout human history. Beginning in the book of Genesis to today, all over the world, from Ireland to the Middle East, to the Hutus and Tutsis, to Mafia wars, and the Hatfields and McCoys. Revenge is handed down from generation to generation, and the toll of human suffering is immense.

Unforgiveness is our way of life. And death.

Deciding to live a life of forgiveness means you're stepping out of the cycle.

Today, I read a story about a young man named Matt, who fell asleep at the wheel and crashed into another vehicle. In the other car was a mom who was expecting her second child. Both she and her unborn child were killed.

Her husband, Erik, is a follower of Jesus. Erik did not go on a revenge tour.

"You forgive as you've been forgiven," he said. "It wasn't an option. If you've been forgiven you need to extend the forgiveness."

According to the story I read, Erik and Matt have now been friends for several years. They hang out at church and get together regularly at the Waffle House. Matt still battles feelings of guilt but says, "I can honestly say that without this friendship, I don't know where I'd be."

For Erik, the refusal to seek revenge, the willingness to put away his right to anger, has made life so much better.

"This has been healing for me too. I've taught on forgiveness, and I know that forgiveness is not so much for the other person but for yourself."[11]

Bingo! This is the ramp off the anger and revenge cycle.

It's not the norm, but "normal" is killing us.

And sure, you might feel like you're "taking a loss" when you forgive. And you know why? Because in a way, you are. You're not going to attempt to tie the score. You're the one stopping the deadly game.

And because of God working through you, that "endless cycle" we're talking about?

It ends.

Can I Be Saved from My Anger? Really?

I love the work of CURE International Children's Hospitals, and I encourage people to get involved. Christians should be eager to help and generous with their money and other resources to heal the poor in Jesus' name. Jesus healed, so can we!

Because humans do human stuff, I get occasional resistance to this whole let's-heal-some-kids thing. Critics say, "But you're using doctors! That's not Jesus-type healing! It's not miraculous healing!"

My first thought is, *Well, if you'd be generous, that would be a miracle.*

But I don't say that. What I do say is this: *There is no non-miraculous healing.*

I mean, if we're defining "miracle" the usual way, as something unexplainable by materialist science, it's true. Science doesn't explain healing at all. We try to describe it but don't truly understand how it works.

Don't take my word for it. Consider the words of one of the most brilliant people on the planet, Iain McGilchrist. He's a neuroscientist, philosopher, psychiatrist, and retired Oxford professor who quoted the British ecological geneticist E. B. Ford in his book *The Matter with Things*. Is this not fascinating?

> When a surgical suture is secured with staples, the resulting repair is conspicuous and crude. Within weeks, the scar is healed, smooth, and scarcely visible. The cells at the site of the incision have identified the nature of the surgical trauma and have initiated maneuvers to restore it. Capillaries re-form so that the microcirculation is restored, innervation is reinstated, and the many epidermal layers are properly reconstituted. *None of this we understand.* These complex processes are invisible to the brain, and are not controlled by cerebral activity, neither are they subject to regulatory intervention by circulating hormones. The cells are the decision-makers.[12]

Think about it: We each have about fourteen trillion cells. They make decisions. We don't understand how these cells make decisions. Where does this intelligence come from?

Oh, we act like we understand, but we don't. We can't heal anyone, really. Like my friend Ben says (he teaches neurosurgery at Harvard), "We don't heal. We treat. It's God who heals."

Exactly. We just get to participate in the process, and only He understands it and animates it.

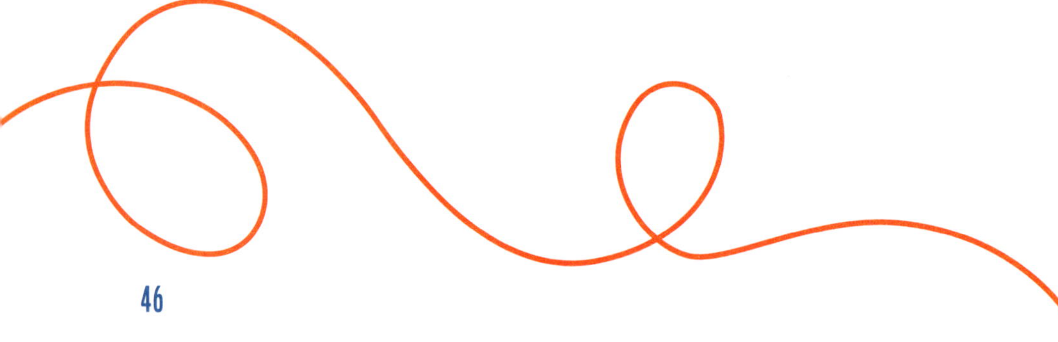

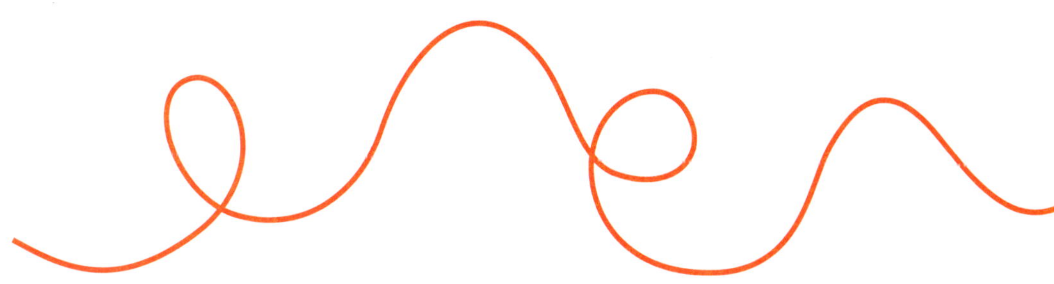

It's all a miracle. Every person, every cell, every time—trillions and trillions of miracles. God is so good at this.

Want to be saved from the sickness and injury of anger? Don't say God can't do this.

By the way: The very word *salvation?* It comes from the word *salve.* It literally means "healing."

And "Salvation," says the psalmist, "belongs to the LORD" (Psalm 3:8 ESV).

Need saving? Need healing? Yes, He can do that.

Healing is His business.

He's not just a great physician, He's the greatest there ever will be.

He can heal you.

This is what He does.

Jesus is Not a Cynic

Every time I read the Gospels, I keep waiting for something to happen, something specific—that keeps not happening. I am waiting for a certain reaction from Jesus.

When the disciples ask Him who's going to get to be His top-ranking, right-hand man in the kingdom of God, I keep thinking Jesus is going to lean in close, place His hands on His beloved friends' shoulders, lovingly look them straight in the eyes, and say, *"ARE YOU KIDDING ME? WHAT IS THE MATTER WITH YOU? I CANNOT BELIEVE THIS!"*

Doesn't happen. Jesus isn't shocked by self-centeredness. Neither is He scandalized by others' immoral behavior. Ever. He knows how we are. He knows how the human heart works.

John 2 tells us, "Jesus didn't trust them, because he knew all about people. No one needed to tell him about human nature" (verses 24–25 NLT). Maybe those who seek to follow Him could take that same approach.

Perhaps a big part of being less offendable is seeing the human heart for what it is: Untrustworthy. Unfaithful. Prone to selfishness. Got it. Now we don't have to be shocked.

Jesus is not a cynic. He's never scornful, hopeless, or jaded. It's purely about growing up enough to recognize just how messed up our world really is and how messed up humans are.

On one level, I understand why people can react with horror at war crimes, for instance. We all intuit, deep down, that something is simply not right about innocent lives being lost. And yet, anyone who reads history knows that war or murder—or injustice in general—is simply not the exception; it's the rule. Moreover, the last hundred years have given us no reason to think things are getting better.

We humans are so persistently naive about this, which is why an article in the satirical online news publication *The Onion* was so spot-on. The headline read, "Neighbors Remember Serial Killer as Serial Killer." When asked about him, his neighbors said he had always seemed like "the serial killer type of fellow."[1]

I probably don't need to unpack that, but here you go, just in case: The usual story is, "I just can't believe he would ever do something like that. He didn't seem like the type." What is "the type" to do something unthinkably horrible? The human heart is capable of staggering evil, and evil people rarely dress in horns and a pitchfork, even if it would make it easier for us to identify them.

I DON'T KNOW

I've learned one great way to be more relaxed and to live at peace is to be quick with this particular phrase, "I don't know."

This is huge for me. I used to want to be Mr. Answer for Everything. I collect facts and figures in my head, out of some weird fear that someone will find me lacking for not knowing the capital of Albania, which is Tirana by the way. I just looked it up.

I know people have good questions about God, including many people who are deconstructing their faith. Why do things happen a certain way? Why does God allow this or that? Most of the time, I just plain don't know. I've learned it's good to say it out loud.

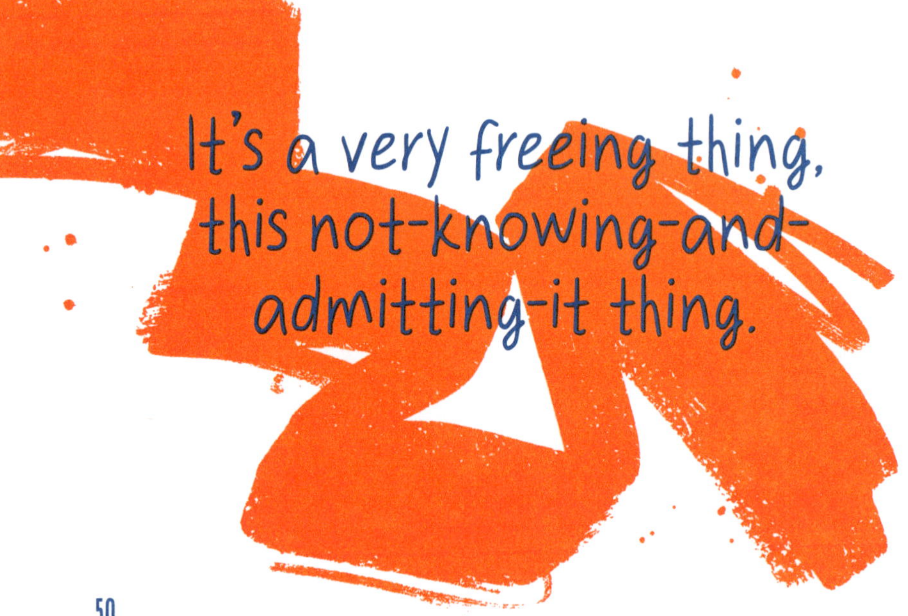

Being at peace doesn't mean knowing and understanding everything. That's a good thing, because we can't pull it off. It means simply trusting the character of God.

My friend Sy wrestled with God. He suffered throughout his life with deep emotional wounds from his childhood. He suffered physically, too, ultimately dying from cancer. But he told me that this is what faith is: having confidence in God's character and capability, knowing that one day your loyalty to God will be vindicated.

"One day I will know the rest of the story that eludes me now," he said. "Therefore, I deliberately choose to continue to be confident in God's character and capability—in spite of unjust circumstances and painful challenges that provoke me to question and doubt."

So yes, I have questions too. Big ones. But I keep seeing reasons to trust God. I keep seeing that style of His at work, how He operates. How difficult or tragic things happen, and there He is at the end of it, proving He was there all along.

I keep seeing how He makes things beautiful.

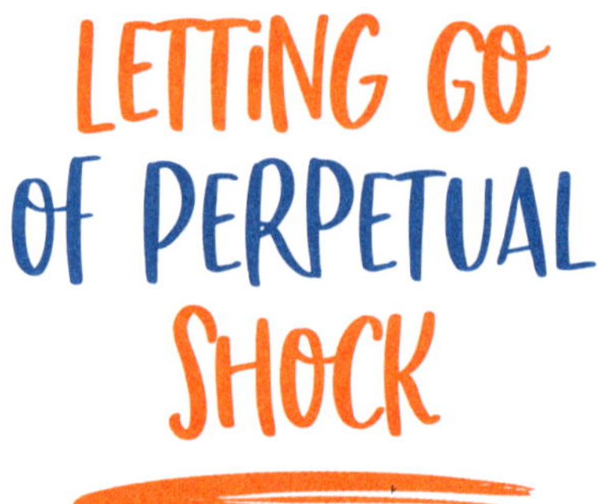

LETTING GO OF PERPETUAL SHOCK

Perhaps you've noticed: Jesus encountered one moral mess after another, and He was never taken aback by anyone's morality. Ever. I can't find any stories (maybe you can find one?) where Jesus sees an immoral person and says anything like, "Wow! Okay. Well, that really is disgusting. That's just too much."

My wife, Carolyn, and I had a discussion regarding someone we both have known for many years. She said something like, "I can't believe she did that!" and I agreed. We were just amazed by this person's refusal to be honest, and—whoa! Wait a second. We "can't believe" she did that?

She has done exactly "that" for thirty years.

Now that I've noticed it, I hear this so often from our radio callers. "I can't believe my mom did this," or "I can't believe my sister would . . ."

And I ask, "Really? You can't believe it?"

I'm not the smartest guy in the world, but I propose that we shouldn't be shocked and amazed if someone who does that thing . . . you know . . . does that thing again.

So how about taking this idea to all of our experiences: You really *can't believe* politicians would lie? You *can't believe* a preacher would cheat on his wife? You *can't believe* someone would try to steal from you? You *can't believe* a neighbor would set off fireworks at 2:00 a.m.? You *can't believe* a world leader would tyrannize his own people?

Are we going to live in perpetual shock at the nature of man?

MARVEL AT THE GOODNESS

And now we can get to the good part, the reason the Christian worldview is *not* cynicism: *We get to marvel at the goodness that humans often produce.*

Okay, we recognize that we humans are prone to dig in and make excuses for ourselves . . . but then you have that talk with a friend who did something to you, and he actually humbles himself and apologizes?

That's a beautiful thing.

Someone happily sacrifices her own hard-earned money to help a family in poverty?

Gaze at it.

Someone sees that you're burdened in an airport security line and lets you go ahead of her?

Wonderful.

Someone who has every reason to be upset at you just lets the matter drop?

Pause and take it in. It's not the rule. It's the beautiful exception.

True story: A friend of mine who did not believe in God haphazardly drove her car into a road construction worker and cost him his legs. From a hospital bed . . . he forgave her. She now believes in God.

Stunning.

Another true story: A few days ago, there was a funeral for a friend of mine. Jerry was a doctor who served the poor in Afghanistan and in Chicago. After arriving for work at CURE International's hospital in Kabul, he was shot and killed by a rogue Afghan police officer.

I cried when I heard about Jerry's death. It still hurts. I loved him. But I cried again, in awe, when I saw his wife, Jan, forgiving his killer just a day after it happened. "We don't know the backstory," she said.

And Jerry had been working there because he knew Jesus loves the people of Afghanistan.

Amazing.

Yes, the world is broken. But don't be offended by it. Instead, thank God that He's intervened in it, and He's going to restore it to everything it was meant to be. His kingdom is breaking through, bit by bit. Recognize it, and wonder at it.

War is not exceptional; peace is. Worry is not exceptional; trust is. Decay is not exceptional; restoration is. Anger is not exceptional; gratitude is. Selfishness is not exceptional; sacrifice is. Defensiveness is not exceptional; love is.

And judgmentalism is not exceptional . . .

But grace is.

Recognize our current state, and then replace the shock and anger with gratitude. Someone cuts you off on your commute? Just expect it. No big deal. Let it drop, and then be thankful for the person, that exceptional person, who lets you merge. See the human heart for what it is, adjust expectations, and be grateful, not angry. When you see, in the midst of all this mess, beautiful glimpses of God's kingdom, defined by love, breathe it in.

Dumpster Church

There once was a pastor, in the days before the internet took off, who availed himself of adult magazines when his wife wasn't around. He knew what he was doing wasn't right, of course, but he did it anyway.

His wife left for a few days on a trip, and once she was gone from their apartment, he brought his magazines out of hiding. Later, he was so frustrated with himself and his continuing addiction that he decided, once and for all, to throw the magazines away.

So he did. He took loads of them to the Dumpster, which sat at the base of their apartment's stairwell, and got rid of them.

Sadly—and perhaps you can relate to this—he later wanted them back. His wife was to arrive soon, and the trash hadn't been collected, so he returned quickly to the Dumpster. Struggling, he leaned over the side to reach the magazines, lost his balance, and fell inside, breaking his arm.

He couldn't get out.

It was just him. A pastor, trapped with his magazines . . . bleating for help in a Dumpster.

And that's where his wife found him.

Since hearing that true story, I think about that guy sometimes. But honestly, I don't think about what a loser he is, or what a hypocrite he is. Instead, I wonder if he's still married. I wonder if his wife forgave him. I think about what it might have been like to be so obviously busted, so humiliatingly, crushingly, can't-explain-this-one busted . . . and then forgiven.

And—you knew I was going here—*that's all of us,* if we're honest. It may not be pornography we're talking about, but in one way or another, we're all the Dumpster Pastor. I've found myself wondering what it would be like to be part of a church of nothing but Dumpster Pastors, people who know they've been caught, their lies exposed, and then set free. I think it would be a very, very fun, free, joyous church.

Walk into many AA meetings or Celebrate Recovery groups, and you'll find something like it. You can't join Alcoholics Anonymous and pretend you've got everything under control. When you join, you're saying, "I can't pretend anymore," and you're joining with people who are right there with you. There's something wonderful about that.

Also wonderful: If you're in an AA meeting, no one can walk in and yell, "Aha! I've got you! You're all hypocrites. You see, I know about you, and I'm going to go ahead and say it: *You are all alcoholics!*"

There would be a pause, some laughter, and maybe an invitation to sit down and join them.

There's a lot less stress when you've been found out. Pretending doesn't come so easily. You can't convince yourself that you're not just as guilty as everyone else anymore. You know the truth, and the truth has a way of setting you free.

And that includes freedom from anger.

I think Dumpster Church would be the opposite of an angry place. We don't get angry when we've just been let off the hook.

It's just conjecture, of course, but I'm guessing, if you were driving home after being forgiven of a capital crime, you're going to let people merge in your lane without yelling at them.

When you're living in the reality of the forgiveness you've been extended, you just don't get angry with others easily.

I suspect our sense of entitlement to anger is directly proportional to our perception of our own relative innocence. So when that illusion is blown up, irrevocably, publicly, in our faces, it's very, very difficult to be angry with someone else.

So yes, as believers in Jesus, remember we've all been exposed publicly for what we are. The depth of our brokenness, the extent of our betrayal, has not only been the subject of news; it's changed history.

When did this public exposure happen? Two thousand years ago, our ugliness was made public on a hill, when a man stripped of His clothing was spat upon, made fun of, abandoned, and executed.

It happened because of us, and it should have been us, but we were let off the hook. When I take that in, both the depth of my betrayal and knowing that my punishment is no longer hanging over my head, I'm downright joyful. I'm extremely grateful.

And, as we already noted, in the human heart, gratitude and anger simply cannot coexist. It's one or the other.

SMOKING STINKS

Maybe you know the feeling: Everyone's doing something you know is wrong, something you find so offensive, but you don't know how to convince them of just how wrong it is. You desperately need to let them know how wrong they are, and how right you are, and you need a means to make a convincing, well-thought-out, thought-provoking, logical argument.

But how? How can you do this? How can you properly impart your sweeping message of disapproval?

It's obvious: Get an awesome T-shirt. I got one that said Smoking Stinks.

I had one of these as a kid. It had a picture of a cigarette with smoke coming out of it, and Smoking Stinks was written in cursive, which made it even fancier.

Most people in our little Illinois town smoked. But as a Christian, I knew smoking was evil, so it was great to finally have a T-shirt that so succinctly communicated my disapproval.

Look, it's simple, folks: You smoke? You stink. I don't smoke. I don't stink.

I win. Questions?

Now, *what,* exactly, do I win? Nothing, as it turns out. But I was a kid, so I have to cut myself some slack. I was just doing what immature humans do, and that is thinking it's my job to put people in their place. I also thought it was my job to single-handedly "win souls for Christ," and when these souls saw my impressive purity and how I abstained from worldly things, like cigarettes, they'd say something like, "Wow! I want to be like you. Tell me about this 'Jesus' who claimed to be the Jewish Messiah, the fulfillment of all prophecy, the hinge in the history of the universe, and who has inspired you to wear this Smoking Stinks T-shirt."

Just for the record: To date, exactly zero people have said that. But it's not too late.

THE KINGDOM OF GOD IS NOT ON DEFENSE

I used to think that to be Christlike meant to be alienated and put off by the sin of others. *Refusing to be alienated and put off by the sin of others is what allows me to be Christlike.*

Recently, I saw an article in a mainstream online magazine about the hip-hop artist Lecrae, who's an outspoken believer. Lecrae loads his music with thoughtful reflections on all aspects of life, including—and especially—the good news of God's love for us. The article read:

> "Christians have no idea how to deal with art," Lecrae said more recently, during a September speech to Christian leaders. "They say, 'Hey Lecrae you can't do that. That's bad. That's secular. You can't touch that. Hey Lecrae, your engineer is not a Christian. He can't mix your stuff. He's going to get sinner cooties on it."

"This is real. I wish I was making this up," he said.

Yeah, me too. I wish he were making that up.

The writer of the article went on to explain this mindset to a mainstream readership, and I think he nailed it.

> Evangelicals adopted an isolationist mindset for much of the 20th century. Non-Christians, the thinking went, carried sin like a virus, and the point of following Jesus was to remain as pure as possible. Christians established their own communities, educational institutions and music festivals, separate from the rest of the world.[2]

Again, I wish it weren't true, and not just of evangelical culture generally, but of myself specifically. I used to think it was not only prudent but my duty to be offended by others' sins. Somehow, I took the example of the King of kings, who wanted to be with us so much that He lowered Himself to be born in a barn full of animals and manure, and I thought it meant I was supposed to raise myself above and away from the messy lives of others.

I guess I thought I was always on defense, guarding myself against the contamination, as though my heart weren't already contaminated with my own self-regard.

Worse, perhaps, I think I bought in to the idea that God and the Enemy are equals, caught up in the classic melodrama of evenly matched good versus evil. It sounds about right, with God on one shoulder and Satan on the other, whispering into our ears, one telling us to be nice and the other telling us to be selfish. (I'm not sure where I got that idea, but it may have been the noted theologian Fred Flintstone.)

But the kingdom of God is not on defense.

I used to read, in Matthew 16, where Jesus was talking about the "gates of hell" coming against the church and how they would not prevail against it, and I'd think, *That's great! We can stand up to the worst attacks.* But that doesn't make any sense. Gates don't attack. I'm kind of a military history nerd, and I still missed this. This reference isn't defensive at all. It's about being on offense. What it actually sounds like is this: Jesus is sending His followers out to love others, and they can go anywhere, even through the gates of hell, to do it.

I have to throw in this caveat, or people will use it to miss the whole point: Yes, it's true, if you are weak in a particular area, you are wise to set up boundaries in that area. Someone who is addicted to alcohol may wisely decide not to go to a bar. But let's stop aspiring to be "weaker brothers" or letting outlier scenarios give us an "out" from venturing into people's lives. Love people where they are and love them boldly.

The Ultimate Pay-It-Forward

Have you done the "pay-it-forward" thing at a drive-thru?

You're in line at, say, Taco Bell, and the Taco Bell window-guy tells you that the lady in the car in front of you already paid for your meal. You say, "That's cool! I'll pick up the tab for the next people," and so on.

Sometimes it can go for hours and dozens of cars and then the local TV people show up for a feel-good story, and everybody gets warm feelings and everybody enjoys their Crunchwrap Supremes™ and I think to myself *What a Wonderful World.*

The idea is simple: You respond to kindness you've been shown—by extending it to others.

Whoa: I just looked up "longest 'pay-it-forward' chain ever" and it happened at this Dairy Queen in the super-nice town of Brainerd, Minnesota. It went for two and a half days and nine hundred cars(!) full of super-nice Brainerd people before some guy finally said, *"No, I will not be participating in this heartwarming event, just fork over my Dilly Bar."*

I bet that guy wasn't really from Brainerd. But that's not the point, which is this: Forgiveness is the Ultimate Pay-It-Forward.

I receive forgiveness. I grant forgiveness.

I tell people frequently to decide, at the beginning of the day, to *forgive people in advance.* We might as well. We know what humans are like, right? We know they're going to do human stuff. As King Solomon said, there's nothing truly new under the sun.

Forgiveness can become a posture, a way of viewing the world. It's not merely a one-off decision here and there. It can permeate our personality.

Of course, when it does, our personalities are different. We'll be changed, which is the whole point. This is what it means to "put on the new self, which is being renewed in knowledge in the image of its creator" (Colossians 3:10 ESV). If we do this, we will look and act more like Jesus.

The Lord, after all, started this forgiveness chain, and we are up next. "Forgive as the Lord forgave you," Paul wrote in Colossians 3:13. And again in Ephesians, right after he told us to get rid of all anger: "Be kind to one another, tenderhearted, forgiving one another, as God in Christ forgave you" (Ephesians 4:32 ESV).

I can forgive ahead of time because I'm already thankful for what God has done for me. It's like knowing, every single morning, that I'm going to get in that drive-thru lane. My meal is already paid for, and I'm going to happily pick up the tab for the family behind me.

This forgiveness thing is a way of life.

This may be obvious to you, but I only noticed this last week, and now I can't unsee it: The word "forgive" itself contains the idea of giving grace ahead of time.

Forward.

Giving.

I don't deserve it, but He forgives me. Maybe you don't deserve it, either, but I'm forgiving you anyway.

DON'T CONDEMN THE CULTURE; REDEEM IT.

I love what author Mike Yaconelli once wrote: "Christians do not condone unbiblical living; we redeem it."[3]

In the book *Messy Spirituality,* Yaconelli told a story about a small group of American soldiers during World War II who sought out a burial site for one of their fallen friends. They were pulling out the next day and were hoping to bury him in a fenced churchyard cemetery nearby.

As the sun was setting, they approached the house next to the church and knocked on the door. The priest answered. They asked him if they could bury their friend in the cemetery.

"I'm sorry," he replied, "but that's only for members of our church."

The priest went on to tell the soldiers they could, if they chose, bury their comrade near the cemetery but on the other side of the fence. They were saddened but had few options, so that's what they did.

The next day, they wanted to visit their fellow soldier's grave site one last time before moving on. When they came to the churchyard, they were shocked: They couldn't find his grave.

It simply wasn't there.

One of them went to the parsonage door and knocked.

"What happened to the grave we dug?" one soldier asked when the priest answered. "It's not there. We did it last night, and it's not there."

"It's still there."

The soldier was baffled.

"You see, last night, I couldn't sleep," the priest confessed. "All I could think about was what I'd told you, that you couldn't bury your friend inside our fence. I regretted that. So, last night, I got up—and I moved the fence."[4]

I now want to be that guy who moves fences. I want to be the guy who says, "Yes, I see the mess you've made of things, just as I have. But God wants us, mess and all. No matter what."

And the good news, too, isn't that God is disinterested in what we do, that He doesn't care how we behave, or what we do to ourselves or others. It's good news that He does care about those things.

So He's going to change us, and if we want the status quo, we don't want Him. But that's not a guilt trip. His desire to change us is just further evidence that we matter to Him, and He loves us.

My goal with relationships is no longer to try to change people. It's to introduce people to a God who is already reaching toward them, right where they are.

This changes everything. It means everyone is welcome, and not just theoretically, but really: Everyone—no matter what their political or religious beliefs—is welcome in my home, at my table.

I happen to be a pro-life, limited-government Jesus-follower. So you're an atheist and a socialist who's pro-choice and thinks Jesus is for losers? Fascinating! Say, how do you like your toast? Tell me more about your thoughts about Jesus and losers . . .

Welcoming people into our lives isn't "glossing over important issues." Refusing to be angry about others' views isn't conflict avoidance or happy-talk. It's the very nature of serving people. I don't pretend the differences aren't there; I just appreciate that God has a different timetable with everyone.

And yes, I've seen wonderful things happen as a result of this newfound patience with people, things like great conversations and changed lives. But that's not even the point for me, because I'm not responsible for changing people's lives. I'm responsible for faithfully loving them. As a believer, that means pointing them to a God who dearly wants them, and for whom I happen to know they yearn.

I don't control anyone, because that's God's job. That's His deal. I can just enjoy and love people. As I keep saying, I wish I would've known this sooner. I wish I could've seen the entire redemptive, narrative arc of the Bible, rather than cherry-picking a few bits that seemed, when isolated, to suggest disengagement with sinners. But the good thing is, I've finally learned:

Don't condemn the culture; redeem it.

I'M NOT CHERRY-PICKING

So, overall, how does Scripture, which is well acquainted with injustice, describe anger?

Well, anger is described as "fierce" and "cruel" in Genesis 49:7. It's "burning" in Exodus 11:8. In the same book, it's also described as a "blazing fury," and if you're not careful, it can "blaze against you" (Exodus 15:7; 22:24 NLT).

In Leviticus 26, anger is something given "full vent" and equated with "hostility" (verse 28 NLT). In Deuteronomy 7, it is associated with the words "burn" and "destroy" (verse 4). In 1 Samuel 20, we see an anger that "boil[s] with rage" (verse 30 NLT). Anger "will not be quenched," according to 2 Kings 22:17. In 2 Samuel 6, it "burst[s] out" (verse 8 NLT); in Job 4, it "blast[s]" (verse 9); and in Job 16, God Himself, in anger, "tears" and "pierces" (verse 9 NLT).

Anger is terrifying and fierce in Psalm 2:5. It's burning and consuming in Psalm 69:24, then smoldering intensely in Psalm 74.

In Isaiah 9:12, it's associated with a fist poised to strike. In chapter 30, it's demonstrated with flames, cloudbursts, thunderstorms, and hailstones (verse 30). In Isaiah 63:3, it tramples.

It doesn't exactly chill out in Lamentations. The words "engulfed" and "slaughtered" are used in chapter 3 (verse 43 NLT).

I'm not cherry-picking. There just aren't lots of references to anger in the Bible as something wonderful. And yet we're now told it's a "gift" for our use when we feel it's "reasonable."

We're also told we should be aroused to anger when we see one of God's commands being broken. Really? Then we're going to be busy . . . really, really busy. We're also going to be really, really angry, all the time—and that's just at *ourselves,* for starters.

Maybe I'm supposed to be angry that often, and maybe it's really a gift. Maybe it'll make my life more joyful and peaceful . . . so long as I don't also mind the burning, blazing, cloud-bursting, striking, thundering, hailing, tearing, piercing, trampling, slaughtering, boiling, and the occasional blasting.

If this is, in fact, what we're supposed to do—experience "righteous anger" whenever we're made aware of one of God's commands being broken—we'll be precisely what the world doesn't need and largely believes we already are: a bunch of uptight, seething hypocrites.

The Bible directs us to get rid of anger (Ephesians 4:31; Colossians 3:8), but our idea of "righteous anger" turns that directive on its head: We can actually pat ourselves on the back for being offended and embracing anger. And all that boiling, piercing, corrosive power becomes part of our lives—and destroys us.

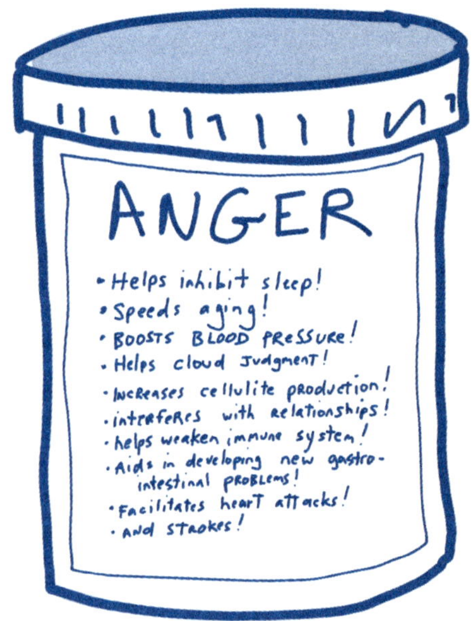

you know, your anger could interfere with your sleep.
6:05 PM

OOH... THAT TICKS me OFF!
6:05 PM

OOH... THAT STILL Ticks me OFF
3:15 AM

A QUICK WORD ABOUT LOVING YOUR ENEMIES:

AND ALSO DUMPING HOT COALS ON PEOPLE'S HEADS

If your enemy is hungry, give him food to eat;
if he is thirsty, give him water to drink.
In doing this, you will heap burning coals on his head,
and the LORD *will reward you.*

PROVERBS 25:21–22

If your enemy is hungry, feed him;
if he is thirsty, give him something to drink.
In doing this, you will heap burning coals on his head.

ROMANS 12:20

Some observations:

- The Bible, which clearly says you should love your enemies, also says you should do it because it'll be like heaping burning coals of fire on their heads.
- This doesn't seem like a loving motive. More like revenge, really, because
- Yikes.

Are we really supposed to feed our hungry enemies to make them feel like their heads are on fire?

Why no, actually. This is one of those instances known as "more context needed" things. It turns out the coal-on-heads thing is actually really wonderful:

In Bible lands almost everything is carried on the head—water jars, baskets of fruit, vegetables, fish, or any other article. Those carrying the burden rarely touch it with the hands, and they walk through crowded streets and lanes with perfect ease. In many homes the only fire they have is kept in a brazier, which they use for simple cooking as well as for warmth. They plan to always keep it burning. If it should go out, some member of the family will take the brazier to a neighbor's house to borrow fire.

Then she will lift the brazier to her head and start for home. If her neighbor is a generous woman, she will heap the brazier full of coals. To feed an enemy and give him drink was like heaping the empty brazier with live coals—which meant food, warmth, and almost life itself to the person or home needing it and was the symbol of finest generosity. It's quite consistent, really. Our motive? Love, not vengeance.

Always. And for everybody.

ANOTHER WAY OF LIVING

When our son, Justice, was tiny, he was obsessed with one thing. Only one: He was completely smitten with *garbage*.

Yep, literal garbage. That's all he wanted, all he thought about. He loved trash. He would excitedly point out Dumpsters to us whenever we were driving about.

Trash. That's it. Nothing else.

We even got him a trash video. It was a full hour of trucks moving garbage around at the dump in big piles. He was mesmerized. No plot, no dialogue; just a lot of beeping from trucks backing up. Who knew there was a market for this?

We had hardwood floors, and I remember my wife and I were in the living room, and we heard a dragging sound . . . and there was Justice, beaming, dragging a bag of trash into the room. His love of garbage was inspiring.

It dawned on me that I could make him an offer. I could stand in front of him and offer him a crisp one-hundred-dollar bill for his bag of garbage. I could tell him, "Look, this is way more valuable. Just give me your trash, and I'll give you this hundred-dollar bill! Just hand it over! Give me your garbage . . ."

There's no way he'd do it.

And you know what? You and I are just like him.

We cling to our self-righteousness and can't possibly imagine giving it up. We think it's how we're supposed to live. *Wait: We're supposed to surrender the idea that we know others' motivations? We're supposed to give up thinking we know everyone's spiritual temperature? We're supposed to live without constantly assessing where we, ourselves, stand spiritually?*

We can't even imagine the world could look that way. This is our way of life. Honestly, we're obsessed with self-righteousness, sick with it, all of us.

But our Father is holding out another way of living, entirely. He's saying it's far more valuable. He knows. He made us. He knows we can live better this way. We'll be under less stress. We'll be able to live in the moment. We won't be constantly offended, perpetually nursing hurts. He's telling us to hand over the idea that we know things we don't about ourselves and others, and simply be humble.

MORE JESUS

I've found myself thinking—even if I don't say it out loud—that part of my job as a Christian is assessing where people stand. Therefore, if I didn't try to make this assessment about others, I wasn't taking Christianity seriously enough, or something. I don't know what I was thinking.

What a sweet, sweet relief to not have to do this.

I don't know where people really stand with God. If someone asks me, "Hey, is that athlete a good Christian guy? I've heard he is," I now admit, right here and right now, that I have no clue.

How would I know?

"Hey, Brant, you love U2. Is Bono really a good Christian?"

I have no response for this. You know, I love some of the stuff he does. I'm a fan. But even if I lived next door to him and hung out every single day with the guy for fifty years, I wouldn't know what's in his heart. (Usually, by the way, I think this question really means,

"Hey, Brant, do you think Bono is trying as hard as I am to be a good Christian?")

Jesus had to point out to seemingly upstanding religious leaders that some prostitutes were closer to the kingdom of God than they were. Would you or I have known that?

Let's be blunt: People are able to fool even their own spouses for a very long time. It's happened very recently with a high-profile evangelical Christian leader. Turns out he'd been leading a double life for decades, and his wife was devastated and humiliated at the news.

I don't know, ultimately, where people stand. I know what they need and what I need. I know we need Jesus. That's it. Period. Everybody. All of us. All the time. More of Him. That's all I know.

If people don't really know Him, they need to know Him. And those who do know Him need to see Him all over again. I'm already a believer, but the kingdom of God is so shockingly opposite the way the rest of the world works that I need constant reminding of what it looks like and how good it is.

It's simple, honestly. You can quit trying to assess everyone; quit pretending you know where people stand; quit fooling yourself into thinking you know what others are thinking, what's in their hearts. Let's be humble and admit what we don't know. What we do know is this simple truth: Everyone, pastors and prostitutes, needs more Jesus.

GOD KNOWS HOW WE'RE WIRED

Last night, I talked with a new friend of mine who shared that he's always seemingly been angry. "I spend half of my life with anger," he said. "I've always lost a tremendous amount of sleep because of it."

As I sat at his kitchen table, with his two adorable toddler daughters running around us, he told me that because he's now in recovery from drug addiction, he's had to make amends with people with whom he's been angry. So he called a guy who once beat him up and told him he was forgiving him.

"The guy was amazed, but it really wasn't for him. It was for me," he said.

"And did you sleep soundly that night?"

He laughed. "Yes! Finally! It's amazing how that happens. And you know what? I've found that when I'm not angry, I can finally be in the moment with my wife and kids. Finally. I can just be here. I'm not thinking about what other people did to me."

God knows how we're wired. He tells us to forgive and to get rid of anger. People made in His image would do well to listen. It means everything, not just for us, but for those around us.

Like two sweet little girls, who can now have their daddy in full.

Life is better this way. It's better when we admit what we don't know, realize our own moral status before God, and give up our made-up Right to Be Offended.

We think we want a right to "righteous anger." It takes a tremendous amount of humility, an extraordinary "dying to self" to hand over this desire, this job, this obsession, to God. But He made us, and He knows how we operate best. He says to hand it over.

And He's promising something of value that no one else—and literally, no other religion—promises.

He's promising a release from the constant evaluation, never-ending striving, and relentless assessment of where we, and everyone else, stand.

He's promising a better way of life. He's holding it out to us, saying, "Hand over the garbage;" and He means it, because He loves us, and He has something better to offer.

He's offering *peace.*

START WITH WHAT'S TRUE

People will tell you that the key to ridding yourself of anxiety is to clear your mind. I find the opposite is true. Maybe I'm not doing it right. My mind just buzzes on. I can't seem to shut it down. I wind up getting aggravated at myself, which I'm pretty sure is not the objective.

I think it's interesting that Jesus' approach is the *opposite* of mind clearing. He told us to actively think about certain things. When He told us to consider the lilies, or think about the birds of the air, and how they're not worried, He was giving us something true to think about.

Check out what Paul wrote about our mindset, right after the part about the peace that transcends understanding:

> Finally, brothers and sisters, whatever is true, whatever is noble, whatever is right, whatever is pure, whatever is lovely, whatever is admirable—if anything is excellent or praiseworthy—think about such things. Whatever you have learned or received or heard from me, or seen in me—put it into practice. And the God of peace will be with you. (Philippians 4:8–9)

If I want peace, I need to think about things—the right things, and not just positive-sounding things—and I have to start with what's actually true.

Instead of trying to think of nothing, I think about these sorts of things:

- I'm not in charge; the Lord is.
- He's very, very good.
- He doesn't hate me.
- He doesn't think I'm a loser.
- He knows me better than I know myself, and He loves me.
- I lack nothing; I have everything I need with Him as my Shepherd.

- There's a lot I can't control, and that's not a bad thing at all.
- I don't need to be afraid of a thing.
- He's got the big picture; I don't.
- God has continually been faithful to me during my entire life. He's earned my trust.

And if I don't trust Him, what's the alternative? I don't see many good ones around.

HUMANS ARE WEIRD

We humans are weird. That's not just my editorial opinion. It's a biological fact. We are remarkably unique among all the creatures on the planet. Other creatures feel threatened, just like we do. The big difference, though, is that when they feel threatened, it's because they're being chased by, say, a lion. And it makes sense that they're threatened, since a lion can kill them.

But humans don't need to be chased by a giant cat or wolves or a shark to feel threatened. We don't have to be chased by anybody or anything. We humans are special, because we can manage to feel threatened while being chased by . . .

Absolutely nothing. And amazingly, *that "nothing" is killing us.*

Maybe you've had this scenario happen to you, the "near miss" in traffic. You're driving a car, and another car comes from out of nowhere, you both slam on the brakes, and you narrowly miss each other. You take a deep breath, say something like "Thank God," and then make sure everybody's okay.

But you also notice your whole body feels different. It's been flooded with hormones, specifically adrenaline and cortisol. Your body went into fight-or-flight mode, perceiving a threat. Your heart rate is now higher, and so is your blood pressure, in order to shoot energy into your body. You've got more sugar in your bloodstream now, too, thanks to the cortisol, and that can help your brain think under pressure.

We are capable of imagining threats and staying in a kind of constant, low-grade fight-or-flight mode. We're capable of feeling threatened all the time, by things that haven't even happened and may not ever happen.

We're so smart, we can trick our bodies into physiological breakdown for no good reason.

The effects of our ability to feel threatened long-term are absolutely devastating. We simply weren't designed to handle this. And it's not just ulcers, either, that are the problem. When we're stressed out over the long haul, everything falls apart.

Here's Jesus, two thousand years ago:

> Therefore I say to you, do not worry about your life, what you will eat or what you will drink; nor about your body, what you will put on. Is not life more than food and the body more than clothing? Look at the birds of the air, for they neither sow nor reap nor gather into barns; yet your heavenly Father feeds them. Are you not of more value than they? (Matthew 6:25–26 NKJV)

We hold on to worry because we don't trust God. We hold on to anger because we don't trust God. We feel threatened because we're insecure, and we're insecure because—surprise!—we don't trust God.

When you start practicing it, you realize: Choosing to be unoffendable means actually, for real, trusting God. The sooner we start this, the healthier we'll be. Not just now and not just physically, but long-term and spiritually.

Consider the Stripe-y Horses

There's a terrific book called *Why Zebras Don't Get Ulcers,*[1] and I love telling people about it, mostly because it's so insightful, but I admit it's also because I don't think we talk about zebras enough, but that's just IMHO.

The author is a primate neuroendocrinologist who writes about how humans are the only creatures who manage to worry about things that aren't even threats.

When a zebra sees a lion chasing him, he thinks something like, "*Huh, there's a lion chasing me.*" And WHAM, his whole body undergoes massive internal changes. Adrenaline and cortisol shoot into his bloodstream. His heart rate goes up and his blood pressure spikes. The flow of his blood reroutes away from his digestive system and toward muscles. His breathing speeds up and his metabolism changes markedly. That's just a start.

These changes serve to make him faster. It's the fight-or-flight response, and for a zebra, it only lasts for a moment, and then it's over. One way or the other it's over. That's what that fight-or-flight response is for, to respond to present threats. Over and done.

But humans? We imagine threats that may or may not happen. Possible scenarios that might happen tomorrow at our jobs. Something negative someone could say or might be thinking. Economic catastrophes that might take us down and leave us hungry.

Unlike, say, gerbils or giraffes, we humans traffic in what-ifs, worst-case possibilities, what-that-person-did-to-me-years-ago.

And you know what? It's deadly. We harbor anger and anxiety, and that keeps us operating in this fight-or-flight mode all the time.

The result of this anger and anxiety isn't just a possible ulcer. (If an ulcer isn't bad enough). We wind up wearing it. Our skin displays stress. Heightened cortisol in our system inhibits collagen production, making us look old before our time. It (literally!) causes thin skin. Plus, stress and anxiety cause weight gain.

The list of deleterious effects is long. But just to include a few more: Keeping this stuff in our system impacts our bone health, heart health, stroke risk, and it weakens our immune system. In short, stress and anxiety can and does kill us.

Long before we had professional endocrinologists to teach us this by talking about zebras, there was Jesus, sitting on a hillside, talking about the birds of the air, and how we should take our cues from them.

They're not imagining threats. They're focused on today.

"Can any one of you by worrying add a single hour to your life?" Jesus asks (Matthew 6:27).

What a characteristically brilliant question. The truth is, we can't, but we think we can. Worry gives us a false sense of control. It doesn't work.

Birds know this. We might try to learn it.

"Therefore," he says, "do not worry about tomorrow, for tomorrow will worry about itself. Each day has enough trouble of its own" (Matthew 6:34).

The Way of Jesus is a way of forgiving enemies and releasing anger. The Way of Jesus is about truly trusting God with the future and letting go of worry. And the Way of Jesus is about thanking God continually, turning to gratitude at all times.

No wonder Jesus says His way means rest for the weary.

Anger? Anxiety? That's the way of the world.

And it's exhausting.

PROBABLY THE BEST THREE-WORD ANSWER EVER

Sometimes we get stressed out about nothing. We worry about things that could happen but don't.

But amazingly, we take this one step further. We get stressed out by *less* than nothing.

Here's what I mean: Once I was super-stressed and needed a friend's input.

Don is older and wiser than me, and I told him about my stress as we shot hoops in his driveway. Don isn't chatty and he thinks before he speaks.

"Man, I don't know what to do," I said, before clanking another brick off the back of the rim. "I want to go to grad school and be a professor. I've always wanted that, and I've got the chance. But I have an opportunity to be a manager at the radio station, and that could pay better for the family. Or we could move to Houston for a job at a great station there."

"I mean, it would be exciting to move, but I feel like if we do, I'll never be in academia. And it would be exciting to be a manager. I'd learn a lot," and so forth and on and on before I think I finally finished with, "I just wish God would show me what to do, but I'm clueless. I keep asking but there's no guidance that I can see and I just—what do you think, Don? What should I do?"

His response? He bounced the ball, took a shot, and said three words I will never forget:

"What a country."

What a country. Yep. Didn't expect that.

But it's a perfect answer.

Why? Because I was stressed out and anxious not because of shortages or limitations but because of *blessings*. I was disturbed by my *options*. Most people in human history haven't had many options like "This career? Or that career? This place, or that faraway place? This university, or that university?"

In this case, I was stressed because I was blessed. Realizing this doesn't magically make the stress disappear, but I've found it sure does help.

If you happen to be in a similar situation, I'm not just saying, "Get over it." I'm saying, "Reframe it."

Don did that for me in three words.

Thank you, sir.

THE SECRET WONDER DRUG "BIG PHARMA" WON'T TELL YOU ABOUT

I always wanted to write one of those click-bait-y headlines. In this case, there's some truth in it. Big Pharma or Little Pharma or Medium Pharma or Whoever can't market this.

I mean, imagine a pill on the market that has these proven benefits:

- Significantly reduces anxiety
- Increases positive emotions
- Improves sleep
- Boosts immune function
- Immediately alleviates feelings of anger
- Helps you build stronger relationships
- Helps you handle adversity
- Diminishes feelings of envy, resentment, and even regret
- Reduces symptoms of mental illness
- Promotes cardiovascular health
- Increases feelings of contentment

Sounds great, huh? Now imagine this list of negative side effects: (none).

Warnings: Keep within reach of children. Maybe they'll try it.

Cost of prescription: Zero dollars ($0).

. . . which, under your health plan, makes your co-pay: zero dollars ($0).

. . . or, if you prefer to work with the accounts department on a payment plan, comes to: zero dollars ($0) for 10 years at 9.5% APR.

Seriously, do you think anyone would be interested if this were available?

Oddly, it is available, but not everyone wants it. They'd rather keep their "righteous" grievances, anger, and resentment.

But I'm interested and if you're reading this book, I bet you are too.

The "pill" is gratitude.

GRATITUDE AND THE ART OF LIVING

My mom worked hard to raise my brother and me. In addition to doing all the usual mom-stuff, she worked at an insurance office and made just enough to buy our groceries. We couldn't afford "Froot Loops" cereal with the toucan mascot but we were able to buy, say, "Fruity Hoops" with the little monkey guy and they were almost as good.

My brother and I were caught up in our own worlds, and we didn't thank her enough. I remember how she'd get fed up with us occasionally. She'd say, "You know what, Darin and Brant? I wouldn't mind hearing 'thank you' once in a while."

She felt unappreciated and she needed to be thanked. Totally understandable.

So, does God feel that way? Unappreciated?

And is that why the Bible is so chockful of commands to give thanks and be thankful and all that?

The answer—and I've gleaned this from the finest, most astute, sophisticated theological minds in history: Nope.

No, God does not need to be thanked. God needs nothing. He's fine, thanks.

The be-grateful thing? That's for us.

And it must be important for us too. The Greek word for "gratitude" gets 157 mentions in the New Testament.[2] It's not a subtle theme.

God wants us to be grateful because He wants us to thrive.

Yes, there are people who will urge you to be ungrateful. They'll give you reasons to focus on what you lack, or reasons to harbor anger and resentment. Perhaps they are threatened by your gratitude. They may accuse you of naivete.

Here we are, in a world awash with anger and anxiety, and God wants us to be *thankful?*

Yes, *because* we live in a world awash in anger and anxiety.

Because we need the peace that comes from thanking God no matter what's happening around us. Check out 1 Thessalonians 5:18: "Give thanks in all circumstances; for this is God's will for you in Christ Jesus."

Notice it doesn't say, FOR all circumstances. This isn't "toxic positivity" and refusing to take needed action in life. ("Lord, I thank You that my kitchen is currently on fire, and . . .") It's about living a life in constant awareness of the goodness of God, no matter what.

Why is it "God's will" for us to do this, to give thanks in all circumstances?

He loves us.

Everything He tells us is for our own good. God created us. He's the original artist; He made us in His image, and the art of living originated with Him.

I love this from pastor and author Douglas Webster:

> At the corner of Bloor and Avenue Roads in downtown Toronto, there was a sign just before the Church of the Redeemer that read, "Discover the Art of Living." As one walked west on Bloor, it appeared to be a sign for the church. It was not. It was an advertisement for a new luxury condominium being built next door. The sign captured the wisdom of the age: The art of living is knowing where to live—in a luxury condo—not how to live.[3]

Gratitude is a central theme in Scripture because it's central to the art of living. A truly thriving human is a grateful human.

Thank You, Lord, for telling us so many times, in so many ways, to be thankful.

IT'S NOT AN OPTION

If you need to sell your junky car, let me help you. I'll write your online ad for you. I'm great at it. You might even say it's a gift. I do this on my radio show: You can call in and tell me what's messed up with your car, and I'll instantly make it sound like it's a premium-level option.

"The heater won't come on at all. Then another day, it will."

Intermittent Climate Control System

"Every time I turn on the radio, the lights start blinking and the horn goes off."

Integrated Entertainment Package

"There's seriously a hole in the roof."

Analog Heads-Up Display

"My cat peed in the car, and it smells terrible."

Organically Based Cabin Air Quality System (OBCAQS)

See? I can do this all day. I frame the problem like it's an option. We love options. Options are good!

Most of the time.

Sometimes it's best when we don't have options, right? There are obvious examples, like if bridge engineers thought correct math "optional." Or if surgeons regarded hygiene as "optional." Or if the creators of *The Muppet Show* considered Gonzo "optional."

I shudder. I do not want to live in that world.

So, here's something we who are following Jesus need to remind each other simply isn't optional: forgiveness.

Just today I saw a young widow speak to a full stadium at her husband's memorial service. Millions watched online as she forgave her husband's killer. Countless Christians remarked online that they were surprised by this. And, indeed, to the larger culture, forgiveness is always surprising. It's a bolt from the blue. Who does that?

But for people who take the name "Christian"? Forgiveness is a must. If we're not practicing forgiveness, we're not following Jesus. I respect her, but I'm not shocked. We don't have the option to not forgive, because forgiveness is the foundation of the Christian faith. I hesitate to pick just one Scripture to make the point, but here's Jesus speaking in Matthew 6:14–15:

> For if you forgive other people when they sin against you, your heavenly Father will also forgive you. But if you do not forgive others their sins, your Father will not forgive your sins.

There is no such thing as following Jesus without a commitment to forgiveness. Forgiveness is a lifestyle that a Christian commits to. I'm not saying it's easy, and we learn how to forgive as we do it. Forgiveness changes us, and it becomes who we are.

Without forgiveness, there is no Christianity and certainly no Christians. Like an electric vehicle with no battery, or the plot from *Mission Impossible: The Final Reckoning*, it just makes no sense.

Do I want to join a Bible study on Thursday night?

That's an option.

Do I want to listen to Christian pop music?

That's an option.

Forgiveness . . . ?

Not an option.

WHO REALLY CARES

It's fair if you are presently thinking, *Wait! Are we not supposed to be angry at injustice? Are you crazy?*

We're not. But this does not make me crazy. The fact that I enjoy puppetry when no one else is looking? That makes me crazy. My daily habit of eating an entire loaf of burnt toast every morning for ten years? Yes, that qualifies me. Sure. You got me.

But this? No. It's not as insane sounding as you think.

Yes, it's unnatural, completely against our instincts, exceedingly radical, certainly unfashionable, counterintuitive, and in violation of conventional wisdom.

Yes to all that.

But so is "Love your enemy."

Let's dispense with one idea at the very start of this chapter: that anger and action are synonymous. Often, we confuse the two, thinking that if we're not angry about an unjust situation, we're simply accepting it. That's completely false.

And it's telling, I think, that the two are so frequently conflated. We've so justified anger that we can't imagine doing the right thing without it. Earlier, I quoted an online devotional that questioned whether we actually ever accomplish anything without anger. The stunning thing, as I've talked with people about this, is how common that idea is.

Anger and action are two very different things, and confusing the two actually hurts our efforts to set things right.

Check out X or Instagram sometime. You can see anger all over the place. People upset about this and "taking a stand" on that. This isn't surprising.

Of course, we're all thankful for the right to speak our minds. But here's what's odd about this confusion when it comes to injustice, anger, and action: A recent study found that people who join causes online are not more apt to actually do something—they're less likely to take action.

According to research from the University of British Columbia, if you click "Like" on "Help the Poor Children of Wherever," you're actually less likely to give actual money to help the actual poor children of Wherever. It's "slacktivism" in action.[1] ("Inaction" is more accurate.)

Let's face it: We're positively in love with "taking stands" that cost us absolutely nothing. We even get to be fashionable in the process.

We get to think we're involved, doing something; and if we're angry, we get to say, "My anger is righteous anger." And since it's "righteous" anger, it stands to reason that we're actually more righteous than the people who aren't angry like we are!

The myth of "righteous anger" actually impedes the taking of action, because it lets us congratulate ourselves for a feeling, rather than for doing something. Meanwhile, someone else, someone who didn't tweet about it, didn't get the bumper sticker, and didn't click "Like" on the cause, is actually sacrificing their time and treasure to genuinely benefit the poor children of Wherever.

There's a book called *Who Really Cares* that's about this very thing. It turns out that the people who are often the most indignant voices in protest of injustice are the least likely to part with their own resources to do anything about it.[2]

So often it's true: One person is angry—but it's someone else who takes action.

WHY WE DO WHAT WE DO MATTERS INFINITELY

Doesn't anger help sometimes? Well, sure, sometimes, in the short run, anger can bring about some good things. Of course. But that's not a credit to anger; that's how the world works. The same could be said of practically anything.

Gluttony, for example, provides jobs for people. It doesn't mean gluttony isn't disordered; it's just that I can see how some good things, short-term, can come from it. That said, I rarely hear anyone speak of "righteous gluttony."

Same thing with bitterness: I've talked with some NFL players about this, how bitterness is the drive for some athletes, pushing them to lift weights harder, hit harder, practice harder; and as a result, they make a living. Some short-term good things can come from bitterness.

But simply saying that "good might come of it" does not make the "it" a righteous thing. Someone might be motivated by anger to do something that is otherwise good. But a relationship with God is like other relationships; it's not a moral "Did you do that?" checklist. The condition of our hearts is not a side issue. Why we do what we do matters infinitely.

In 1 Corinthians, Paul said, "Though I bestow all my goods to feed the poor . . . but have not love, it profits me nothing" (13:3 NKJV).

You can recognize injustice, stand up to it, even sacrifice your life fighting it. And you can do it without anger. In fact, you'll do it better. You won't be remembered as angry, but as convicted of what's right, and loving to the very end. This kind of love leaves an impression on one's enemies that anger simply never will.

Confusing Ourselves with God

I once read an article called "The Gift of Anger," about how Christians should see their anger, when justified, as a blessing.[3] And we're given a test in so many of these articles, which is essentially this: to ask ourselves, "Is our anger justified?" If yes, it's justifiable anger.

Nice test. I see what you did there, test-maker people.

Another Christian piece I read says Jesus' story about the unmerciful servant is an example of when we should harbor anger.[4] This is the very story we talked about in an earlier chapter, where God is angry at those of us who do not forgive others, when we ourselves are guilty too. The rationale is, "See, God gets angry in this story. That means we should too!" But that's not the meaning of the story at all. We are not the king in that story. The king's anger does not give the unmerciful servant a valid basis for his own anger.

We are so protective of our own anger that we'll twist that story to justify our anger instead of rid ourselves of it. And it's instructive, given the way the unmerciful servant story is mishandled.

Think about it: In order for us to justify our right to anger, we have to confuse ourselves with God.

If we think the biblical writers didn't anticipate the level of injustice and brokenness in our modern world, we're being naive on an epic scale. Early Christians in many cases were being targeted, imprisoned, and killed. What's more, the Middle Eastern world was shot through with infanticide, slavery, racism, sexism, child abuse, unjust wars and occupations, torture . . . it's all there.

And yet, the early Christians got letters from their leaders telling them to get rid of anger, period. Even if you disagree with me, I think you'll find this is a fair question: If our modern writers are accurate, and Christians really are called to anger against injustice, why is that call missing entirely from these letters?

The early church dealt with injustice daily and was aware of widespread injustices affecting others. So why were they not told to get angry about it, if human anger toward true injustice is actually righteous?

Why isn't righteous anger ever listed among the things that a Spirit-filled life will bring us? If it's righteous, why is it not akin to the "fruit of the Spirit," like love, joy, peace, and gentleness? Why is anger in Scripture so consistently lumped in the other lists with things like, say, slander and malice, with no exclusions for the "righteous" variety? (See, for example, Colossians 3:8.)

We aren't to just pretend anger away or feel guilty for the initial emotion of anger. But we are to deal with it, with the goal of eradicating it within us. This, of course, is not easy to do, but it's not complex to understand, either.

How to Pray for Enemies: Some ProTips™

You don't have to be an expert.

You can start right now. Think of someone who antagonizes you. Or maybe, it goes deeper. Maybe it's someone you can't imagine rooting for, no matter what.

An "enemy" needn't be your sworn archnemesis who laughs maniacally while ruining your life from their Icy Lair of Evil. It might just be an annoying person on social media. At times, there may be numerous people you perceive to be opposing you in different ways.

Hopefully, you have someone in mind now. So how do you pray for an enemy? What do you even say?

Great questions! Here's where I step in with ProTips™. I'm not a "pro" at this. I'm just learning too. But it's cool to say "ProTips™":

Pray that God would give them peace.

Note: Do not pray that they would REST in peace. That's trying to game the system. Seriously: The person antagonizing you is probably not at peace, even if they seem to have it all together. Maybe he or she has never known peace in their lives. Pray that your enemy will experience the deep "shalom" peace in their homes that comes from knowing God.

Pray they will be surrounded by people who know God.

I've seen this happen. Suddenly, they keep running into people who know the peace of God. People they genuinely respect. This is huge, because arguments rarely change people's minds, but relationships do.

And a great thing about this: When I pray this for people who bug me, I'm reminded I'm not the solution to their problems. I'm not who everyone needs. Jesus is.

Pray God will have mercy on them.

You're now interceding for your enemy. This is a profound thing, indeed. Jesus did this on the cross when He prayed, "Father, forgive them, for they know not what they do" (Luke 23:34 ESV).

Praying for our enemies reorients our focus and reminds us of the grace we've been given. Why would we pray for mercy for someone who doesn't deserve it? Because we didn't. Thank You, Lord.

Pray that God will heal your anger toward them.

I'm convinced this is a prayer God will answer. I'm sure of it, in fact, because He loves us. He doesn't want us saddled with anger. The cost is too high. Of course, as I've written, He tells us to pray for our enemies because it's good for us to move past our anger and get back to life-giving stuff.

Will my enemies repent? Will they see the error of their ways? Will they humble themselves? Will they apologize to me?

Maybe. Maybe not. But that's not up to me.

What's up to me is that I'm loyal to a God who has had mercy on me and wants me to extend mercy to others. Being merciful is one of the ways I can become more like Him.

Try this praying-for-enemies thing. Even now, please. Do this for your enemy this very moment.

If you're anything like me, as you do it, you may sense a difference in your feelings toward them.

As you pray, your heart will slow down and your blood pressure will drop. You may even sense your heart leaning toward them, like you're now genuinely rooting for them.

This is doing what Jesus told us to do.

It's called *obedience.* It changes us, even heals us, because everything Jesus tells us is actually for our own good.

STEPPING OUT OF ANGER

Dallas Willard said we now have so many angry Christians simply because "they're not taught out of it."

Few ever present the radical implications of what it means to die to ourselves and what it means to practice a lifestyle of forgiveness. "Stepping out of anger," Willard says, "means you are surrendering your will to God. It means you have accepted that you don't have to have your way."[5] When I've read commentaries on Ephesians 4:31, where Paul says to get rid of bitterness, anger, evil speaking, and so on, the commenter very often inserts the word *unreasonable* before anger. But that's not in the text, and the commenter doesn't extend the "unreasonable" standard to anything else on the list. (What about "unreasonable bitterness"?)

"But didn't some biblical heroes act out of anger?" Well, sure they did. They were humans. I'm so thankful the Bible is not a just-so story, not a singsongy, children's pop-up book of SuperClean Heroes. Its stories are of people, like us moderns, who lie and cheat and steal and harbor anger and occasionally even kill innocent people. It's a mess. To say, "Well, Moses got angry at injustice in Exodus 2" is not to say that we should kill Egyptians too.

Those stories aren't how-to templates for our lives; they're stories that point us, ultimately, to the goodness of God.

WAITING IS REVOLUTIONARY

Feeling powerless is sometimes excruciating. We want justice, and we want it now. If we can't get it, we can at least harbor our self-righteous anger. Sometimes, it's all we think we can do.

The Bible tells us to do something truly revolutionary, certainly un-American, and completely at odds with that: *Wait.*

> Wait on the LORD; be of good courage, and He shall strengthen your heart; wait, I say, on the LORD! (Psalm 27:14 NKJV)
>
> For evildoers shall be cut off; but those who wait on the LORD, they shall inherit the earth. (Psalm 37:9 NKJV)
>
> Wait on the LORD, and keep His way, and He shall exalt you to inherit the land; when the wicked are cut off, you shall see it. (Psalm 37:34 NKJV)
>
> Do not say, "I will recompense evil"; wait for the LORD, and He will save you. (Proverbs 20:22 NKJV)

This is really, really, really, really, really hard. I know; I just wrote *really* five times, and that's pretty unprofessional, but I could've written a lot more. I know it's hard, because it's hard for me right now, and yet, there it is. *Wait!*

And if I'm overemphasizing by writing *really* a lot, the writers of the Bible emphasize *wait* far more. I picked just a few verses of dozens. Waiting is not a subtle theme of Scripture.

And yes, we're also told to be just and to love mercy, in the meantime: "The LORD has told you, human, what is good; he has told you what he wants from you: to do what is right to other people, love being kind to others, and live humbly, obeying your God" (Micah 6:8 NCV).

Living "humbly" is the part I'm so often missing in my anger. I want comeuppance for the proud, and I want it now. I don't want to wait.

In fact, I don't fully trust God. I'm worried He won't handle things the way I'd like.

Worry and anger often go hand in hand. They're both about feeling threatened, and they both represent, ultimately, a lack of trust. But there's a flipside, and it's good news: We get to see all over again how freeing it really is to trust God.

My anger isn't a sign of trust; it's the very opposite. I'm worried someone's going to get away with something, like God's not noticing and it's all up to me. This kind of anger is perfectly human, of course, and perfectly natural, and just as perfectly destructive as any other kind of anger.

> Rest in the LORD, and wait patiently for Him; do not fret because of him who prospers in his way, because of the man who brings wicked schemes to pass. Cease from anger, and forsake wrath; do not fret—it only causes harm. (Psalm 37:7–8 NKJV)

So let's joyfully work for justice and mercy. And while we do it, let's trust that God, our Father, who actually loves us, and also loves mercy and justice more than we ever could, is ultimately going to set things right. We don't need to act like kids who've been abandoned and are forced to take matters into our own hands, defending ourselves at every turn. Our Father is coming home, and He tells us, over and over, He's going to take care of things.

Outsource Your Worries

I was reading a book about being efficient and getting things all the way done. I got only about halfway, but I do remember something: The author offered tips on getting help by outsourcing.

He'd hire people in other countries, and they'd take care of his stuff, everything from dealing with clients to setting up dental appointments.

He was under a lot of pressure, and as a kind of joke he asked his assistant in India to worry for him. He gave her a list of a few things he was worried about, and she said, "Okay, I'll worry about those things for you today."

What's even weirder: The guy said it worked! Just knowing someone was out there, somewhere, worrying in his stead? It somehow put him more at ease. He would set those things aside and concentrate on things he could control that day.

This is kind of goofy, but that's how our minds work. We want some sense of control over the future, and at some level, worrying gives it to us. Maybe paying someone in India to worry for you can give you that same sense.

But there's an even better way. "Outsourcing our worries" may be an absolutely brilliant way to think about our trusting relationship with God. I mean, it's scriptural.

The verse literally says, "Give all your worries and cares to God, for he cares about you" (1 Peter 5:7 NLT). Throw them to Him. Let Him deal with them, instead of you.

We can hire someone in India to do it for you, and that apparently has a bit of benefit. But imagine handing it over to someone really powerful, like, say, the Creator of the universe. He can do things!

This sounds like a very good deal. I need to do this more. I'm learning just how helpful it is in having peace. As I learn He's truly good, and believe the things about Him that Jesus believes, I trust Him more to handle things.

Jesus Was Not a Crazy Man

Speaking of control: We love it. We want it so bad. We can't imagine being without it. Even when we can't have it, we want to pretend we have it.

I have seen empirical evidence of this on vivid display. It happens when humans gather to upend club-shaped wooden objects arranged in a triangle on the floor. You grab a heavy ball and roll it down a long, varnished runway in hopes of knocking them over. It's called bowling, and it starts with renting shoes other people have just worn and I'd never really thought about that until I put on a pair and they were still warm and I don't want to think about this anymore really.

The fascinating thing, beyond that we're willing to do the gross shoe-rental thing, is what happens once humans release the ball. We lean and gyrate and gesticulate and turn, even though it has no effect whatsoever on what's happening. I mean, the ball is gone. We should really let it go.

In life, it's really better if we just do what we can . . . and then outsource the worry. We did our thing; now, Lord, please do Yours.

Psychologists say we think worrying will help us be more prepared for something catastrophic or make us better at solving a problem we're facing. But neither is true, they say. We're just leaning over and hoping that helps steer the bowling ball toward the pins. Jesus, who knows a thing or two about how we function best, told us that worrying is a waste:

> Therefore I tell you, do not worry about your life, what you will eat or drink; or about your body, what you will wear. Is not life more than food, and the body more than clothes? Look at the birds of the air; they do not sow or reap or store away in barns, and yet your heavenly Father feeds them. Are you not much more valuable than they? Can any one of you by worrying add a single hour to your life? (Matthew 6:25–27).

Jesus was not a crazy man. He was not being idealistic. He was telling us how to live. He knows what He's talking about.

LIKE THE BIRDS

"As long as we are worrying," James Bryan Smith wrote, "we can't seek first the kingdom of God. As long as we are seeking first the kingdom of God, we can't worry."[6]

But again, what about the evils of government? What about injustice? What about persecution? What about unfairness? What about poverty? What about racism? What about wars? What about infanticide? What about misogyny? What about illegal government occupation? What about all the immorality? What about all the oppression?

Was Jesus unaware of these things when He told us not to worry?

No, Jesus was not unaware of these things. Neither was His immediate audience. It was all part of their lives, all part of the first-century Roman world. If Jesus had been born into our current setting, I doubt He would change His tune and go with "Oh, wow. Yeah, okay, now *this* is seriously messed up. You have some legit worries here. Yikes, you guys."

If anything, I imagine people in the first century A.D. had more to worry about. For starters: Their life spans were shorter. The food supply was far more uncertain. They didn't have vaccines or antibiotics. And yet there Jesus was, telling people to trust God. Be like little animals. They're just concerned about today and what's directly in front of them. You'll have troubles, remember? But be of good cheer.

Lately, when I start feeling stressed about something that may happen tomorrow or next week or whenever, I picture sitting at a desk and having someone hand me a package that says "The Future" on it. And this mail is glowing. For some reason I have a Geiger counter on my desk and it's ticking. This thing is radioactive.

So I say, "Hey, this isn't for me. Not my department." So they take it away to the Radioactive Mail Department that easily and expertly handles that stuff. The future is not my deal. Not my department. I'm about today's stuff. Next!

Maybe it's a simplistic or goofy little image, of course, but it helps me. I have to remember: "Not my department. Not my department." Over and over. "Be like the birds," Jesus said. They don't kid themselves about how powerful they are or that they control the future.

THE "MAN IN THE CAR PARADOX" AND CARING LESS WHAT EVERYBODY THINKS OF US

It's called the "Man in the Car Paradox."

I will now explain it, but I know what you're thinking: *"Brant, can you explain it with haiku?"*

That's an odd request, but okay:

If I had cool car

People wouldn't like me more

They'd just want my car

Morgan Housel popularized this paradox in his haiku-free but otherwise excellent book *The Psychology of Money.*

It's that simple. We see a cool car and think, *That would be amazing to have that car. I would have fun driving it and people would think I was cool.*

Notice what we don't think: *Wow, whoever owns that car must be amazing.*

Same thing with a nice house. We're thinking, *Wow, I'd love to live in a house like that.* We're not thinking, *Wow, I admire and respect whomever lives there.*

Again, it's a similar thing with posting our curated vacation photos. I can show my awesome "golden hour" self at sunset in Santorini, but I better realize it just makes people think, *Hmmm . . . I could see myself in Santorini,* not *Brant is a wonderful person.*

(By the way, good luck getting a selfie in Santorini without forty thousand other people crammed into the background also getting selfies.)

Santorini nights

Humans crammedlikethisgoodgrief

Send helicopter

Sorry. I can't seem to stop now.

The point is, our culture is all about spending our time, energy, and money to manage what others think of us. Why didn't more people "like" this? How many nice comments will this get? Why didn't this person respond? What is that person implying? Why did this person post an unflattering photo of me?

Scan this QR Code to listen to Brant's song, "Take Down That Picture of Me."

Image management is nerve-wracking. For me, it's not limited to social media. It's constant data about whether or not people appreciate what I'm doing. I'm on a couple hundred radio stations, and they all have ratings. ("They liked you last week on KLZZ, and now they hate you, but the folks on WORP think you're okay this week, but . . .") It's a never-ending referendum on my personality.

How do I handle it? I really don't. I can't. It's too much, but it's forced me into a good place: If someone doesn't like me, or if something didn't make the impact I'd hoped it would—that's okay.

I'm not going to attempt to convince people to like me. It's overwhelming. So, I'm waving the white flag. I'm throwing in the towel. I'm doing other metaphorical things with fabrics that say, "I can't manage this."

Great news: The Way of Jesus leads us away from image-concern. Jesus tells us to knock it off with the manipulative language trying to impress people. "All you need to say is simply 'Yes' or 'No'; anything beyond this comes from the evil one," He says in Matthew 5:37. The people listening at the time were prone to using fancy oaths to impress people with their religiosity. It was image management, and Jesus wants to set us free from it.

This is something I'm still growing into, and I'm happy to report that it leads to less anxiety and less anger. I'm less frustrated when I'm taken out of context or when someone says something that makes me look bad. I feel less threatened that someone will steal the spotlight.

A Poem:

you want my spotlight?
that's seriously okay
for real I'm good thanks

ON THE SIMPLE LIFE, AND ALSO THE 4,893 MUST-HAVES YOU NEED RIGHT NOW

There's a magazine called *Real Simple*, and I like that name because I like real things and also simple things. So, I'm on board.

But I'm not sure how simple it is. Like this article I just saw: "22 Easy 4th of July Menu Ideas for the Ultimate Backyard Barbecue."[1] I guess I would make it twenty-three because they didn't include "just grill some meat.."

Here's another helpful website article: "46 Affordable Travel Essentials."

Forty-six *essentials*? What, am I having stevedores crane my steam trunks onto the *Queen Mary*?

This one is my fave. It's a headline I saw to help us guys: "7 Colognes You Should Be Wearing Right Now."

Seven colognes.

Right now, gentlemen.

Start spraying.

Anyway, it's true that in our culture, even the simple life is just another way to sell you more and better stuff. They won't tell you, ever, about the true Ultimate Life Hack. It's The Thing That Must Not Be Encouraged.

Contentment.

"I have learned to be content whatever the circumstances," Paul writes from, of all places, prison. "I know what it is to be in need, and I know what it is to have plenty. I have learned the secret of being content in any and every situation, whether well fed or hungry, whether living in plenty or in want" (Philippians 4:11–12).

And then the apostle Paul says this:

"I can do all this through him who gives me strength" (verse 13).

That last line is a popular verse. Most people don't realize Paul is talking about being content.

I tell younger guys all the time, one of the most powerful mindsets you can have is this, when you encounter an expensive truck or the latest phone or see someone else's pricey vacation: "Wow, that's really awesome—and I don't need to own it."

I can appreciate something without thinking, *I need to make this mine.*

If you want to practice this mindset, I recommend memorizing Paul's words above, or (this is way shorter) try Psalm 23:1. It's truly, radically countercultural. It won't make you a great consumer, but as you internalize the truth of it, it changes everything:

"The LORD is my Shepherd, I lack nothing."

(Psalm 23:1)

If you put your trust in Him, you have everything you need for what faces you today.

That sounds like fluffy religious talk, but it's real and it's simple and it's the deepest kind of true.

That Awesome Thing? Doomed. Next?

I bet this freaked out the young guys who were following Jesus:

> As Jesus was leaving the temple, one of his disciples said to him, "Look, Teacher! What massive stones! What magnificent buildings!"
>
> "Do you see all these great buildings?" replied Jesus. "Not one stone here will be left on another; every one will be thrown down" (Mark 13:1–2).

I know this is momentous theologically and historically. But for some reason, it's kind of funny to me. Like:

Delighted young guy: Wow!! Check this OUT!!! So cool!!! It's HUGE, and—

Jesus: It's doomed.

Probably not that funny to anyone else, which honestly makes things funnier to me. It reminds me of watching a cereal commercial during a football game with my friend Chris, who was then working on his PhD in nutrition.

TV ad: And now, it's fortified with beta-carotene!!!

Chris, (disgusted): Oh yeah—like it's not going to be COMPLETELY ISOMERIZED by the time it hits the bowl.

I still laugh about that. Niche humor, I'm sure. Indulge me.

Really though, imagine: Marveling at the seeming permanence of a structure. This is going to last forever, right! This is important! Surely, this is perma—

Nope.

It looks like it's going to last, sure. But it's not going to last.

Just today I heard a history podcaster, talking about all the wars triggered by royal succession in history. He said, "Nature abhors a vacant throne."[2]

Ain't that the truth. And it's not just true in terms of historical power intrigue, it's true for us as well. There will be no vacant throne in our hearts. We will make someone, or something, or some cause, the king of our lives. It could be just about anything: money, travel experiences, career, politics, prestige, music, the NFL, our appearance, kids, or a particular influencer, whatever—but the throne will not stay vacant.

Something will be our Ultimate.

Humans find things to worship. We'll carve something out of a tree if we must.

Here's something that occupies the throne for a lot of us: our security. It's the Ultimate Thing, even lurking behind a possible veneer of Christian religiosity. Any hint of major change, or potential suffering for us or our loved one feels overwhelming and intolerable.

This is so human, so relatable.

But unlike the Fruit of the Spirit, the god of security does not yield peace. The fruit of this god is not joy, that "pervasive sense of well-being, regardless of circumstances."

No, that only comes from when I put my hope in the Lord.

Not my money.

Not my comfort.

Not my status.

. . . and not even my country.

Think about Psalm 121. Most people think this was written by King David during a dangerous journey. He had armies at his disposal. He had fortresses. But he knows where his ultimate hope comes from, and doesn't mention any of that:

> I lift up my eyes to the mountains—
> where does my help come from?
> My help comes from the Lord,
> the Maker of heaven and earth (Psalm 121:1–2).

My help must come from the Lord. Ultimately, if my hope is in anything else, it's a horrible mistake.

I remember tucking my sweet daughter, Julia, in bed when she was little, and so full of worries. Julia wanted me to promise her nothing would happen to me or her mom.

I wanted to promise her that. I couldn't promise that.

But I could tell her this: *I trust the character and goodness of God.* If we trust Him, in the end, no matter what happens, we'll be with Him and we will be alive and well and happy and together. He promises it.

Honestly, I don't know how people who don't trust God answer their kids' questions. I'd really struggle with that.

The longer we walk with Jesus, the more we'll say, "I had many questions and doubts, but I'm so glad I trusted Him."

"Nature abhors a vacant throne," and so does human nature.

In the end, and even now, who—or what—occupies the throne of your heart makes every difference.

There It Is

I knew this one was to be about the love of God, and I wanted to write it while on some kind of "spiritual high" so I could somehow write about it poetically, and it would just flow or something.

I really did. That was the plan. But that's not happening, apparently. I haven't felt particularly spiritual in a long time, and that's not out of the norm for me, for a lot of reasons. And now, I'm wiped out from a difficult week at work, and I'm particularly aware of my own sinfulness too. So I'm asking God to have mercy on me as I write this, and to help me anyway. Maybe it's for the best, since—I'm now convinced of this—most people who genuinely want to know God are not living in a persistent, perpetual state of amazement at His love.

And yet, His love is amazing. And His love is persistent and perpetual and unrelenting, even as our emotions, and our attention spans, aren't. The goodness of God is not dependent on my attentiveness to it. It does not come and go, wax and wane, or suddenly vanish like my misguided, untrustworthy emotions.

We're just not very attentive, honestly.

We're all a little bit like Dug the dog in the 2009 movie *Up*—kind of airheaded. We can sing "Amazing Grace" and be taken by it all, by the sweeping scope of God's love for all of us, His willingness to forgive us, and His desire to know us, and His unending—Squirrel!—and how He loves us in spite of our—Seahawks game today!—and

"His grace will lead me . . ."—I forgot to email that guy—"We've no less days to sing God's praise than when we've first begun" . . . and I totally smell coffee; is someone making coffee? And you know what? God's grace is still amazing. We can ignore it, let it slide from our awareness, and yet . . . there it is.

AMAZING WHAT LOVE DOES

One time, a real nice lady gave me a real nice plant for my office . . . and I done killed it. It was tall and lush and green and full and beautiful, and I gave it the ol' Extreme Makeover, Neglect Edition, and turned it into a crusty brown pile of detritus in a pot.

I didn't know where to throw it out. So after I killed the plant, I put the pot formerly known as "plant" out on the veranda, which is a commons area for all the organizations in our building. That way, no one would know who abandoned the pot-o'-nothing. I'm a class act.

The radio studio shares a wall with the veranda. I looked out the window during the show one morning and noticed this prim, bookish, middle-aged lady—someone I still haven't met—watering the dead plant. Naive but, you know, sweet. But mostly naive.

She came out and did this every single day. I'd be on the air, notice some movement to my right, out the window, and there she was, watering and trimming the dead plant.

And then the dead plant, which Brant Hansen killed, started growing. The dang thing started shooting up green. It grew and grew, and she kept trimming it, too, here and there. She kept watering.

One morning, I looked out and marveled: That plant that I, Brant Hansen, personally killed, was now more beautiful than when I had it in my office. It was back, better than ever. Glowing healthy! And it occurred to me . . .

I could take my plant back now.

It would look great in my office! I'll just go snag it sometime when no one's out there and bring it back in—you know, liven up the office for the me-meister!

I mentioned this to my wife, Carolyn. She said it wouldn't be right to take the plant back. She said it wasn't mine anymore. She said that lady redeemed it, so it's hers now.

Amazing what love does.

Just Today

In the morning, Cozy and I go for a walk.

I don't want to be gross, but just so you know, on these walks one of us stops to make a mess. The other one of us puts that mess in a bag. In this way, we complement each other. Cozy and I have real synergy. We know our roles and have them down, cold. I don't think we've ever—not even once—got them confused.

And as we head out, just a Dog Dad and his fluffy golden retriever, I talk to God.

This is the dog. Please retain photo for your files. Thx.

And when I talk to God, I talk out loud, and I ask Him for my daily bread. And by "daily bread," I mean just the things I need *today*. I know He's got the big picture. I know He can and will make a path for me.

So, what do I need today? It depends on the day. But most of the time, since I'm introverted, I need social energy. So I ask for that.

If I'm doing my radio show that day, I know I'll need about twenty things to say. That's daunting, because I'm always starting with zero, and wondering how I could possibly come up with twenty more. So, I ask Him to give me things to say that are genuinely valuable to people.

And He helps me. Every day, after the show, I am drained. But I'm deeply thankful and a bit amazed that I got through it.

I ask God for help with specific meetings I've got scheduled, and for the patience I might need for such-and-such person.

I ask Him to protect me and my family from evil.

I ask Him to increase my influence with people, but only to the extent that I'm conveying His kingdom accurately and well. Otherwise, forget it. I don't want any influence.

I'm being vulnerable by telling you this stuff. I know authors and radio people need to be good self-promoters. I'm just not into it. I feel silly. Other people have a genuine gift for it, and it can be a good thing. But I don't want the pressure of entering the social media fray or "getting my name out there." So, I pray about it.

Lord, will You help with that? Make a way for me, somehow. Give me things to say, and if You want, places to say it.

I talk with Him about my family and ask for His blessing on specific people in my life.

I think of people whom I particularly struggle to love (including people I don't personally know, like media figures and politicians) and I ask Him to bless them and their families with peace.

I sometimes think about the neighbors in the houses that Cozy and I walk by, and I ask for peace in their homes, and that they would come to know Him.

I don't remember all these things every time. But you get the gist. It's all pretty simple stuff.

Sometimes I'll recite verses, like my longtime fave, Psalm 143:8 (KJV), because it's perfect for mornings, and so perfect for a guy like me, who has always struggled to fully believe that God could deeply love him.

> Cause me to hear thy lovingkindness in the morning,
> for in thee do I trust:
> Cause me to know the way wherein I should walk; for I
> lift up my soul unto thee.

In the end, like Dallas Willard was fond of saying, prayer is just you and God talking about what you're doing in life together.[3] So I do that.

It's astonishing that God wants to partner with us, but He does. He always has. He'll walk with us.

Cozy enjoys walking with me, although she struggled at first. She'd pull and tug and try to go her own way. But she's a grown-up fluffball now, and we're in sync.

Of course, Cozy can't possibly understand what I'm talking with God about. Her doggie thoughts are not mine, and mine aren't hers.

But Cozy trusts me. She knows I'm for her. I provide for her. Cozy doesn't have to worry about next week or what might happen next year.

Cozy knows I'm even willing to clean up her stuff.

There's a great analogy here. I didn't even plan it. It just worked out that way.

Cozy only needs to focus on what's in front of her. And you know what? That's true of me too.

Just today.

THE GOSPEL OF GRACE

Once, I forgot my keys in a church building, just as a group of us were getting ready to leave. Losing stuff is a lifestyle for me, so I was kind of proud that I remembered I'd left them down the hall and up the stairs, in the kitchen area.

It was dimly lit, but as I was gracefully running down the hallway, I saw a post in the middle. I avoided it deftly and ran to the left side, before athletically darting up the stairs, grabbing the keys, crisply pivoting, bounding confidently back down the stairs, sprinting effortlessly down the hallway—and then smartly slamming my entire body into a plate-glass wall.

I shattered it. With my face.

Apparently, the other side of the post had glass from ceiling to floor. It was reinforced with wire mesh, so I didn't make it through. I just hit it, full sprint, and shook the entire building.

In the emergency room, I remember thinking, *You know, this is interesting. I was 100 percent sure there was nothing there. But there was, in fact, something there. I know this, because, among other observations, I note that I am bleeding profusely. Plus, my face hurts.*

I was completely convinced the hallway was clear. It's funny how reality didn't change to fit my interpretation of things. And by "funny," of course, I mean "only funny, like, ten years later."

Whether or not you currently feel that God is around doesn't alter reality. Whether or not you feel He loves you, or even that you are worthy of His love, doesn't change reality either.

What does this have to do with being unoffendable? Everything. That is, it changes everything if I'm attentive to it. It's the best news ever. Here's how Brennan Manning described the news:

> Because salvation is by grace through faith, I believe that among the countless number of people standing in front of the throne and in front of the Lamb, dressed in white robes and holding palms in their hands (see Revelation 7:9), I shall see the prostitute from the Kit-Kat Ranch in Carson City, Nevada, who tearfully told me that she could find no other employment to support her two-year-old son. I shall see the woman who had an abortion and is haunted by guilt and remorse but did the best she could faced with grueling alternatives; the businessman besieged with debt who sold his integrity in a series of desperate transactions; the insecure clergyman addicted to being liked, who never challenged his people from the pulpit and longed for unconditional love; the sexually abused teen molested by his father and now selling his body on the street, who, as he falls asleep each night after his last "trick," whispers the name of the unknown God he learned about in Sunday school.

"But how?" we ask.

Then the voice says, "They have washed their robes and have made them white in the blood of the Lamb."

There they are. There we are—the multitude who so wanted to be faithful, who at times got defeated, soiled by life, and bested by trials, wearing the bloodied garments of life's tribulations, but through it all clung to faith.

My friends, if this is not good news to you, you have never understood the gospel of grace.[4]

As I said, the best news ever.

YOU ARE OFF THE HOOK

No matter what, God still loves us. He has not abandoned us. Every hope we've ever had—that someone would find value in us, would think we were worthy of love, would find us enjoyable and attractive and pleasing and worthwhile—is met in Him. God Himself loves us! His love trumps everything. And nothing, Paul wrote in Romans, can separate us from that love.

Nothing.

And, he also wrote, if you put your trust in Jesus, there is no condemnation for you. None. You are off the hook. This is so stunning, so hard to actually believe, because nothing else in the world seems to work that way. It's not based on my performance? It's based on what God has done for me? He loves me because . . . He just loves? It's who He is? He's not constantly evaluating my religious "goodness"? He's not angry with me? Seriously?

It's a massive pressure relief. When I take it in, I'm still shocked. Really? I can see where a lot of those old hymn writers were coming from. "Amazing love, how can it be?"[5]

I'm a moral failure whose mind has drifted while even writing the last few paragraphs, with thoughts ranging from silly to immature to rebellious to lazy to selfish. I'm inconsistent to the core. But in a very real sense, it just doesn't matter. I want to grow up, but my Father loves me even as I am.

It's incredible news.

And that matters, when it comes to our offendability. Imagine you open your email and there's actually some great news: Someone wants to give you a hundred million dollars. (Now that I think about it, I get this offer from Nigerian friends on a daily basis. But say this is legit.) Chances are, after getting the money, you won't be quickly offended when someone cuts you off in traffic a few minutes later.

Better example, maybe: You've just been given the news by your doctor that your daughter's cancerous tumor, once thought to be terminal, is nowhere to be found. She's healed. You then notice you have a text message from that annoying guy at work, asking you to cover for him again. Are you angry?

The reality is this: The "good news" is, ultimately, even better. But you and I are forgetful people, and we get distracted, and we certainly don't always live in the reality of it. We need to be more attentive, and having people and disciplines in our lives to remind us of that great news will help us be remarkably slow to anger and offense.

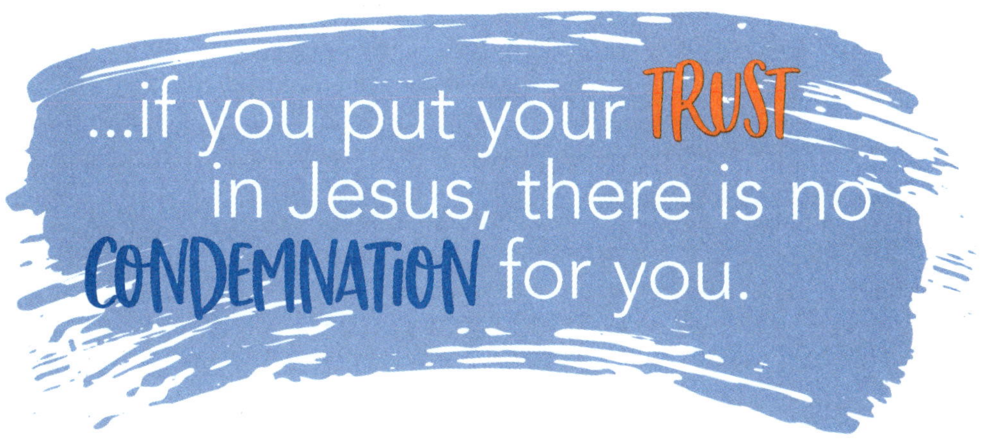

TESTING THE LIMITS

I had a "Groupon" for a sushi place. Do you remember "Groupon"? It was like an online coupon thing.

I'm wondering what happened to it. Is it still a thing? I'm going to check right now and get back to you in the next paragraph.

(insert hold music)

Whoa. It's still a thing. There's still a website and it says, "With Groupon, Fun Never Ends."[6]

Well, I remember when I had a Groupon and the fun ended.

My wife, Carolyn, and I joined our friends Matt and Sherri for dinner at a sushi place. I was proud that I could get us 50 percent off at this sushi place with my Groupon.

Now, I don't like sushi, so I had to find something on a menu that I liked. Ah, there was an appetizer called a "chicken tower." I ordered that, and it was grilled chicken strip-things stacked up like a little Jenga tower-type-deal.

It was good! I told the server, who was a really nice guy, that I'd like another.

And that was good, too, so I ordered another one.

And another one.

And that was good, too, so I orde—

"No."

What? Did you say "no"?

The server gestured toward the kitchen and said, "He say, 'No more chicken tower.'"

Wait. Really. I can't have another?

"He tired of chicken tower. Too many chicken tower."

You're cutting me off?

"No chicken tower."

But I have this Groupon, and—

"He not care about Groupon."

Looking back, I guess I can't blame the guy. Like Mark Twain or maybe G. K. Chesterton probably said, "A Groupon is a powerful, powerful thing but it's not a blank check for chicken towers."

I have a point here, and here it is: Everyone has limits. And that's why God's patience is breathtaking. Take another look at Jesus' story of the Unmerciful Servant. Jesus tells Peter that he should forgive someone not seven, but seventy-seven times. In other words, there's no limit. Then Jesus immediately pivots to the story. Check out how much the guy owes the king:

> Therefore, the kingdom of heaven is like a king who wanted to settle accounts with his servants. As he began the settlement, a man who owed him ten thousand bags of gold was brought to him. (Matthew 18:23–24)

That is an INSANE amount of money. The Greek that's translated here into "ten thousand bags of gold" actually is "ten thousand talents." Scholars say a talent was worth about 6,000 denarii. And how much was a denarius in today's dollars?

About 50 bucks.

So, let's do the math: 6,000 X $50 is $300,000

So, a talent is worth about $300,000. And he owes how many talents? TEN THOUSAND?

Let's see, using my phone calculator, 300,000 X 10,000 is—wow:

The guy owes the king *three billion dollars.*

Now, if you're thinking, *"That's not even realistic,"* well, Jesus is making a point.

Since he was not able to pay, the master ordered that he and his wife and his children and all that he had be sold to repay the debt.

"At this the servant fell on his knees before him. 'Be patient with me,' he begged, 'and I will pay back everything.' The servant's master took pity on him, canceled the debt and let him go" (Matthew 18:25–27).

He cancels the servant's three-billion-dollar debt. Completely.

And why?

Because he asked!

Now, you can read the rest of the story in Matthew 18. But stop and marvel at the grace of God. Is there no limit? He'll wipe out a three-billion-dollar personal debt, just because we ask?

Wow.

Fair warning about the rest of that story: The forgiven servant does not extend forgiveness to someone else, and so he's tortured and thrown in prison.

So, he did find a limit, and this is the scary part:

The limit was the one that he set for others.

By the way, this little essay is not to be read as a veiled message to the chicken tower chef. I totally would have cut me off too.

OUR BEHAVIOR GIVES US AWAY

Here's a problem, and it's based on years of interacting with thousands of self-described Christians: It's not merely that we're not attentive to the fact that God loves us. I suspect many of us actually just don't believe it.

I suspect this because our behavior gives us away. After all, what we believe isn't what we say we believe; it's what we do. And what many of us do, as far as I can tell, is strive and strain and push and pull and work and worry and even anguish to try to somehow win favor with a Father who's already pleased with us. I could spend an hour on the radio, reciting scriptures about how we are now no longer under law, and how, if you've put your faith in Jesus, God has adopted you into His family, and I already know the inevitable response: Christians lined up to tell me it's not really quite true, that the real issue is that we need to stop sinning right now and work harder.

No wonder we get so angry. We're displeased with others because we're convinced God is displeased with us. We "believe" God loves us, but we suspect it's provisional, based on whether we ever get our act straightened out. That's a lot to carry.

If Christians are indeed the most easily offended people on the planet, this burden would go a long way toward explaining why. We're the ones convinced God has six-hundred-plus rules—rules we know we can't keep—and that He's ticked off at us. But we try to keep them anyway. It's a prescription for immense frustration with ourselves.

And then we see other people not trying as hard as we are, and that's downright enraging. We hope God will give them their comeuppance someday, because if He doesn't, what the heck are we doing all this for?

So we believe the "good news," but not really. Not fully. We simultaneously do and we don't. Humans manage to do this with a lot of things. Many of us are a lot like the man in Mark 9, who begs Jesus to help his boy, who's being oppressed by a demonic spirit.

> When [the demon] saw [Jesus], immediately the spirit convulsed [the boy], and he fell on the ground and wallowed, foaming at the mouth. So [Jesus] asked his father, "How long has this been happening to him?" And he said, "From childhood. And often he has thrown him both into the fire and into the water to destroy him. But if You can do anything, have compassion on us and help us." Jesus said to him, "If you can believe, all things are possible to him who believes." Immediately the father of the child cried out and said with tears, "Lord, I believe; help my unbelief!" (verses 20–24 NKJV)

I believe; help my unbelief! I just said that many of us are like this father, but maybe that's not true. Maybe we're not as honest as he was. So let's match his transparency before Jesus and admit we struggle with this.

And we can, because—get this!—Jesus didn't blast the guy. Instead, He made his dreams come true. There's no, "Are you kidding me? You *still* don't fully believe?"

Jesus set the boy free, and a father got his child back. No lectures, no diatribes.

Tea and Cookies with a Very Old Lady

Of all the Bible characters, Miriam doesn't get mentioned much. We should talk more about Miriam.

Miriam was Moses' older sister, and wow, did she see it all. First, she watched as her helpless baby brother was put in a basket in the reeds of a river to avoid being put to death by the Pharaoh. The kid had no chance, right? Then, Miriam saw Moses be rescued by the daughter of the evil Pharaoh himself. Now, what chance does he have? They'd been found out!

Then—we're skipping a lot here—fast-forwarding some eighty-plus years later (!) she watches as that same little brother leads his people out of slavery. Instead of her baby brother drowning in the reeds, years later, Miriam sees Pharaoh and all his men drowning in the Sea of Reeds. What a turn of events!

And, at ninety years old, Miriam leads all the women into spontaneous singing and dancing.

After all is said and done, the Lord is faithful.

Who saw THAT coming?

If we could sit down for tea with old-lady Miriam, I wonder what worries we could talk to her about.

Maybe we'd talk about family issues, money problems, how messed up our country is, or why the world feels so hopeless—or whatever.

Miriam would probably be a patient listener, but I suspect we'd stop ourselves midsentence. She'd possess a knowing look, I think—maybe a little pity mixed with bemusement, like she knows we don't need to be worried.

Miriam would give us "the look" because she knows how this all ends, and we need to know it, too, and we should really believe it.

So maybe I'd ask her to remind me: How does all of this end?

I've seen some beautiful things, so much of the world. I've seen little kids get to run and play for the first time. I've seen moms cry tears of joy. I've seen my own kids grow up and become my friends. So much goodness.

But there's an ache to life. Even remembering all the things I went through as a kid—the trauma, fear, and heartbreak. So much pain in the world feels overwhelming if I pause and think about it. And terrible things can still happen.

How can any of this make sense? I can't get my head around it. What is this about? How does this end?

And maybe she'd say, "Don't be afraid. Just stand still and watch the Lord rescue you today."

And maybe we'd believe her.

Maybe we'd start believing we are safe, after all. Why didn't we see it all along? After all, Jesus told us we'd have troubles but to "be of good cheer." We could have been of good cheer all this time!

Miriam had to sing her own song.

So do you.

I wonder what your song will be.

I wonder what mine will be too.

One thing I'm sure of, when it's all said and done, it'll be the motley lot of us, the formerly broken and seemingly hopeless, the formerly paralyzed, sick, and heartbroken, former strugglers and sinners and bumblers. All of us together.

And we'll be dancing.

I can't wait. In fact, I'm starting now.

THE KING WANTS TO BE WITH US

In Khaled Hosseini's magnificent book, *And the Mountains Echoed*, one of the characters, Nabi, reflects on the latter days of his life as a driver and butler in Kabul, Afghanistan, and the lives of those he's served. After a long recounting of pain, love, hardship, and hurt, Nabi says, "I suspect the truth is that we are waiting, all of us, against insurmountable odds, for something extraordinary to happen to us."[1]

That has a ring of truth about it. I've sometimes caught myself repeatedly checking my email, for instance, with a vague sense of hope. I've had to ask myself, "What, exactly, am I hoping is going to pop up in my email?" I'm not sure. But I'm hoping for something new, some good news, from someone. I want something extraordinary to happen. I may be alone in this, but I don't think I am. We're all checking for some news, out of habit, even. We're mindlessly doing it, mechanically reaching for our phones, and hoping . . . for something.

Like Nabi, I think we're all waiting, all yearning, for something that will change everything. Something remarkable, indeed, that makes us, finally, amazingly significant and completely secure. We're waiting for something extraordinary.

My question is, What if that extraordinary thing has already happened?

What if we knew that the King wanted to be with us, wanted us in His family, His home . . . forever?

SETTING ASIDE OFFENSE

My radio show's producer, Sherri, is African American. She just got back from a trip where she was a guest speaker at a youth event in a church that was primarily white. Just before the Sunday morning service, she was called into the minister's study for prayer, and she met a man who was overtly hostile to her. The way he looked at her, dismissively and contemptuously, made her feel hated. She felt utterly unwelcome, lonely, and out of place.

After she spoke, the same man approached her, took off his glasses, and started crying. He told her that hers was the most influential talk he'd ever heard, and it had affected him particularly because he is very racist against Black people. She was stunned by his honesty.

"We've always been this WAY. My FAMILY has always been racist. I've LEARNED this from my dad. I'm so SORRY. I've got to change," he told her. "I can see JESUS is using you. And He's using you to CHANGE ME."

Sherri then asked to meet his dad. She did. And she hugged him.

I know Sherri takes racism very, very seriously. But, she says, she also has to forgive racists, because she has to love people in her family. And they are part of her family. She has to love them as Jesus loves her.

Sherri's love is not naive. But that's exactly why it's so profound. She's setting her offense aside, not because it doesn't matter, not because it isn't completely understandable, but because of what Jesus has done for her. She's choosing against offense, not just because God loves these men but also because God loves her and has set aside her very real offenses in order to be with her.

There are those of us who pat ourselves on the back for loving our families and friends. "I'm loyal to the end; I'd die for my kids," we'll say. Truth is, that's not really terribly remarkable. Everyone, or practically everyone, feels this way.

What *is* terribly remarkable is when someone is willing to love a person, in the name of Jesus, whom they would otherwise despise. It makes no sense otherwise. Why would we ever regard someone as family who would otherwise be an enemy? Why ignore his faults, or cover her wrongs with love?

Without Jesus, it simply makes no sense.

Sherri's very refusal, and our very refusal, to take and hold offense is evidence of the existence of God.

This is how they'll know we belong to Him, Jesus says. So let's love—from this moment forward—because He first loved us.

Forgiveness Means Sacrifice

Letting go of offense and anger means forgiving, and forgiveness means sacrifice. This is what's so striking to me, as I get older, about Jesus: I'm simultaneously dumbfounded that I'm "off the hook" because of what He's done for me, but still stopped in my tracks by what's being asked of me.

It's both. I know God has already forgiven me. And yet this very truth obligates me. It means if someone has done something to wound me, I have to endure a second hurt, one that feels like another wound. My sense of justice says the person who hurt me should pay; but with forgiveness, it's the forgiver—the victim—who must pay again.

This will probably seem like a silly story, but I'll share it anyway. When I lived in South Florida, I had a surfboard. (This makes little sense, given that I can barely balance myself on dry land, but that's not important now.) My wife loaned it to some friends. They destroyed it and didn't offer to pay for it.

At that moment, I had a choice: Forgive them, and I, and my sense of justice, take the hit; or refuse to forgive them and try to make them pay for it. In either scenario, someone pays.

I'm actually not going to tell you the end of the story, because it doesn't matter. Whenever there's an injury to a relationship, a hurt, a broken heart, or even a broken thing, and you are willing to forgive, you are saying, "I got this. I'm going to pick up the bill for this."

This is, of course, precisely what God has done for us.

Our anger is valuable to us. That's why we want to hold it, to savor it. It means something. It means we've been wronged, we're in the right, and we're the victims in an unfair exchange. We want to even out the scales, and one way to do it, at least psychologically, is to stay offended.

Since anger has value, giving it up requires a sacrifice. And, as we've explored, it's one that's simply not optional for the follower of Jesus. The cross simultaneously stands as a constant reminder of His willingness to "pay the bill" and as an indictment on us when we are unwilling to do the same for others.

WALKING AWAY FROM JESUS

There's a story in Luke, where an apparently "good," religious, and rich young man approached Jesus, wondering what he must do to inherit eternal life. Ultimately, Jesus placed a demand on him—sell everything and give to the poor—and we're told the young man heard that and walked away, sad.

I think for many of us who live in this society that is so riven with anger, even addicted to it, Jesus is giving us a similar demand: "Give up your anger. Because of what I've done for you, give it up, and forgive."

Sadly, our response is, "That's not fair." And we walk away too. One thing that strikes me about the rich young man story: Jesus doesn't leave him with room to wriggle. The man will either do what Jesus says, or walk away. There's no splitting the difference, paying lip service, or trying to split theological hairs.

But we love to do this with forgiveness. Jesus tells His followers to forgive as we have been forgiven, yet we find reasons why this doesn't quite apply in our situation. (Maybe He didn't anticipate what I was going to have to endure . . . Does He realize what He's asking?) But we don't walk away sad, like the rich young man.

Instead, we tell ourselves that we can live a Christian lifestyle and integrate our own decisions about whom to forgive, and when. This is especially dangerous, because when we do that, we're walking away. But we're not aware we've walked away at all. We've just de-radicalized the very nature of following Jesus, because we think we know a better way.

HAPPY BIRTHDAY, AGNES!

Once upon a time, there was a prostitute. She lived in Hawaii, and it was her birthday. Her name was Agnes. Tony Campolo writes about her in his book *The Kingdom of God Is a Party*.

He was in a diner in Honolulu, very late one night—three thirty in the morning, actually—when he couldn't sleep from jet lag. It was just him, his donut and coffee, and the guy behind the counter, when suddenly, a group of prostitutes came in. They sat down on either side of Tony, and they were very crude and very loud. He was about to leave.

But then he overheard one of them saying tomorrow was her birthday, her thirty-ninth. Another woman made fun of her for bringing it up. "What do you want, Agnes, a party? You want a cake? You want us to sing 'Happy Birthday'?"

Agnes said no, she didn't. She'd never had a party, or a birthday cake, so why start now?

> When I heard that, I made a decision. I sat and waited until the women had left. Then I called over the fat guy behind the counter, and I asked him, "Do they come in here every night?"
>
> "Yeah!" he answered. "The one right next to me, does she come here every night?" "Yeah!" he said. "That's Agnes. Yeah, she comes in here every night. Why d'ya wanta know?"
>
> "Because I heard her say that tomorrow is her birthday," I told him. "What do you say you and I do something about that? What do you

> think about us throwing a birthday party for her—right here—tomorrow night?"[2]

The guy behind the counter—his name was Harry—loved the idea, and so did his wife, who did the cooking in back. In fact, he wanted to make the birthday cake. Tony told him he'd be there earlier the next morning, in time to decorate. And he decorated, complete with crepe paper streamers and a sign that read, "Happy Birthday, Agnes!"

Apparently, word of the party got out, because the place was filled with prostitutes before Agnes's arrival. When she came in at three thirty with a friend, the whole place erupted, "Happy birthday!"

She was stunned. Mouth agape. "Flabbergasted," Tony writes. Her friend had to steady her. And when they began to sing, she began to cry.

Harry lit the candles, and as she blew out the cake, she was in tears. She didn't want to cut it. Instead, she asked if she could keep it a little while. She wondered if that would be okay.

Harry said she could. Then she said, "I want to take the cake home, okay? I'll be right back, honest!" She left. Everyone was stunned silent. Tony said he didn't know what else to do, so he broke the silence with, "What do you say we pray?"

> Looking back on it now, it seems more than strange for a sociologist to be leading a prayer meeting with a bunch of prostitutes in a diner in Honolulu at 3:30 in the morning. But then it just felt like the right thing to do.
>
> I prayed for Agnes. I prayed for her salvation. I prayed that her life would be changed and that God would be good to her.

When I finished, Harry leaned over the counter and with a trace of hostility in his voice, he said, "Hey! You never told me you were a preacher.

"What kind of church do you belong to?"

In one of those moments when just the right words came, I answered,

"I belong to a church that throws birthday parties for whores at 3:30 in the morning."

Harry waited a moment and then almost sneered as he answered, "No you don't. There's no church like that. If there was, I'd join it. I'd join a church like that!"[3]

You know what? I have a new rule: I won't join a church that doesn't do that. Because that's the Jesus I recognize, the One who mends the brokenhearted and is never, ever scandalized by sinners. The Founder of my faith gave us new rules of engagement. He was told, like everyone else in His society, to stay away from lepers. He wouldn't do it. Sure, it made people mad that Jesus was flouting their rules. But He didn't stay away from lepers. Instead, He touched them and made them whole.

How love operates

I really do feel that God is helping me grow up. The things Jesus said make more sense to me now, and I understand better what Paul wrote about getting rid of all anger. The point isn't that we were justified in our anger. The point is freedom—freedom to love. Freedom to have God-given sight, the ability to look at that highly offensive someone and see what is not yet, as though it were.

We're made for it, so we'll find it both exhausting . . . and exhilarating.

Henri Nouwen was a priest. He also had plenty of what the culture considers "significant": He was a brilliant writer and a professor at both Yale and Harvard. As he lived his life, he saw the struggle between operating by the values of the world and the values of the kingdom of God:

More and more, the desire grows in me simply to walk around, greet people, enter their homes, sit on their doorsteps, play ball, throw water, and be known as someone who wants to live with them. It is a privilege to have the time to practice this simple ministry of presence.

Still, it is not as simple as it seems. My own desire to be useful, to do something significant, or to be part of some impressive project is so strong that soon my time is taken up by meetings, conferences, study groups, and workshops that prevent me from walking the streets. It is difficult not to have plans, not to organize people around an urgent cause, and not to feel that you are working directly for social progress.

But I wonder more and more if the first thing shouldn't be to know people by name, to eat and drink with them, to listen to their stories and tell your own, and to let them know with words, handshakes, and hugs that you do not simply like them, but truly love them.[4]

Loving people means divesting ourselves of our status. We're not being naive in doing it. We've surrendered it for good reason, believing that there is something better in exchange. We decide to be unoffendable because that's how love operates; it gives up its "status" entirely.

THE REMEDY FOR AN INFLAMED EGO

I want to talk about your elbow precisely because you're not thinking about it right now. That is, at least until I mentioned it you weren't thinking about your elbow, unless you just injured it, or it's bruised or inflamed or something. If there's something wrong with it, sure, it's on your mind. That's the point.

I have some kind of shoulder issue at the moment, and if I move it much at all, or something touches it, it hurts. (Yes, I should go to the doctor for this, but (a) I'm a guy, and (b) I'd rather just search online and come up with the worst possible medical scenarios and freak myself out. This is my plan.) Because of the inflammation, I'm acutely aware of my right shoulder. I'm always thinking about it, adjusting for it, even changing my plans to avoid hurting it.

Timothy Keller used the idea of favoring an inflamed joint to make a great point: This is precisely how the human ego works. It "hurts" when it's inflamed. Sure, it's always there—everyone's got an ego—but when it's oversized, it's constantly being injured or threatened. When it's "all about me," I'm constantly aware of myself, bracing myself for ego injury.[5]

Real humility isn't about putting yourself down or pretending your performance is substandard at everything you try. Real humility lies in self-forgetfulness.

Few want to hear this, but it's true, and it can be enormously helpful in life: If you're constantly being hurt, offended, or angered, you should honestly evaluate your inflamed ego.

When you're humble, you're not constantly thinking, *How do I look?* or *Am I a success?* or *What do they think of me?* It's just not on your radar screen. When self-interested thoughts do cross your mind, you're able to recognize them for what they are, in most cases: downright silly.

GOD FAVORS THE UNDERDOG

Once, a friend invited me to a fancy conference in Washington, DC. I really had no business there. But I found myself in this hotel suite, where they were having a reception for some leaders from African governments. The suite had one of those lunch meat 'n' crackers–type spreads out. Since I have poor social skills and like crackers, I spent a lot of time in the lunch meat 'n' crackers area.

Anyway, I overheard this lady, who was going from government leader guy to government leader guy, explaining what God had told her to do, which was to save the world. That was her mandate, and she told them she was going to start small: with Africa. She had a Big Vision, and she was going to do this and that, and then this other thing, and then this would happen, and she had it pretty much mapped out. It was awesome.

I like people who can rescue everybody, so I thought to myself, *That's cool,* and then I noticed they had those fancy Pepperidge Farm cookie-stix things. I also noticed she moved on to the next guy and talked a lot again about what she was going to do. She had some big plans that involved her doing some significant stuff. Pretty neat.

It was lunchtime, so I made my way to this big lunch area downstairs, where they had more crackers. The lunch organizers had arranged for a young married couple to speak. The guy never spoke, actually. His wife said he was more of the computer-nerd type, and she was nervous, but she'd talk, since they asked.

She is a Jesus-follower who had gone to Africa (Africa, again?) a while back for a few weeks. She made some friends there who didn't have much of anything. When she came back, she asked God to help her help them. And she got an idea: She and her husband scanned their wedding guest list into their computer and asked those folks to loan their African friends some money. Her husband set up a website so their wedding friends could loan the money and make contact with the people they were giving to.

She didn't know what else to do. This couple was heartbroken for a few families, and she knew God loved them. They had no Big Vision, just love for a few people she knew, and she wanted to help them start businesses so they could have some way to live.

God blessed their efforts.

They've now helped more than a few people. They've helped hundreds of thousands. More than a million people have loaned money through them, and it's added up to more than five hundred million dollars.

She said they didn't really know what they were doing—they just loved a few people. She doesn't understand how this happened, she said, except she thinks God made it happen.

I didn't walk away from that lunch impressed at how amazingly talented the couple was. Instead, I thought about how God loves us and how He favors the underdog.

NO ANT IS A SUPERSTAR

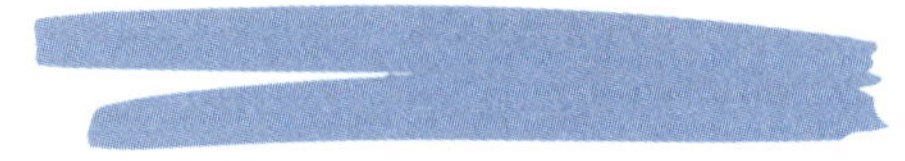

I suspect that we, like the lady in the suite, put a lot of pressure on ourselves to be something significant, and anything that gets in the way of that, or threatens that significance, threatens us.

I've noticed, too, that Christians are especially good at wrapping our significance in Christian terms, in ministry terms, to avoid the impression that we're self-centered.

But it's still about us. We're not content with what God has done and is doing, and we want the Big Story to include us in a starring role.

Or at least we want to follow someone we think is in a starring role. We like big visionaries, big planners, big capital-*L* Leaders. (Maybe this explains why, in Christian bookstores, there are frequently ten times as many books on "leadership" than about following.[6] Given that we are called to be disciples and follow, that's a little awkward.) There's just more cachet there. We want to be significant.

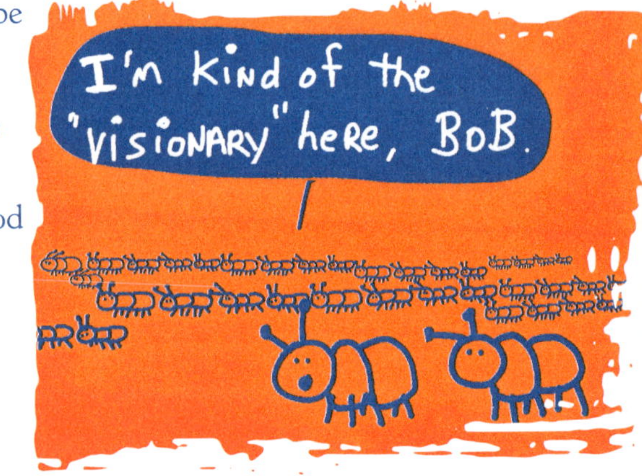

The Bible, on the other hand, is shockingly devoid of Awesome, Big Planner People. Instead, God continually chooses the least likely to be chosen, the broken and the humble. It's clearly His modus operandi.

I've heard this response from people when I talk about this idea: "But how can we possibly get things done without big-time visionaries? Without massive plans to save the world?"

Well, the Bible actually singles out a specific, heroic animal species to illustrate how to get things done. If you want to know how to do it, don't go to the soaring eagle. Don't go to the impressive, roaring lion either. God may have a different idea:

> Go watch the ants, you lazy person. Watch what they do and be wise. Ants have no commander, no leader or ruler, but they store up food in the summer and gather their supplies at harvest. (Proverbs 6:6–8 NCV)

Yes. Watch how the ants operate. They get it.

Sure enough, modern research shows just how remarkable ants are. They all know what to do and when to do it. They know when to rest, when to battle intruders, when to take care of their eggs, all of it. If there are too many ants foraging, just enough ants decide to quit foraging and take on other jobs.

They know how to build massive anthills that are marvels of construction engineering.

And they do it all without a hierarchy. They manage it all without management. They get it done without any one ant knowing the "big picture." No ant is a superstar. No ant is irreplaceable. How they operate is still somewhat mysterious to science, but scientists do know that ants just use the information that's in front of them, and then they respond. That's it. That's all the information an ant has.

The Bible singles out a species wherein every individual member does whatever needs doing, just by responding to what's in front of it. An ant can't worry about the big blueprint. No ant actually has the big picture. If they each do their thing, the thing right in front of them, the big picture takes care of itself.

I can't help but think, as much as we humans value our visionaries, that God loves the way the humble ant operates. And as in the case of the young couple who designed a website because they wanted to help some people they loved, it's God who has the Big Picture.

I also can't help but think that if we just responded to things God places in front of us in our lives, and entrusted the visionary role to the Lord Himself, beautiful things could happen. It doesn't mean we don't need leaders; of course we do. But we need humble ones, leaders who don't need a spotlight, don't need approval, and don't need attention.

"Ant" leaders who prod us on and serve us in order to help free us to do what God puts in front of us.

EMBRACING RADICAL HUMILITY

I get the impression from reading the stories of the Bible that God really enjoys making marvelous things happen, using the humble. I think it's because then it's obvious who, exactly, made that marvelous thing happen. If anything wonderful happens in my life, and I'm humble, it'll be apparent that it didn't happen because Brant is an amazing visionary. It happened because God will use anybody with a willing heart.

And when people look at what happened, they won't walk away feeling disempowered because they'll never be as awesome and talented as I am. Instead, they'll be encouraged to serve God boldly, because, again, He used Brant, so He'll use anybody!

Of course, humility is not about timidity, and it's not about self-denigration.

I love C. S. Lewis's description:

> To even get near [humility], even for a moment, is like a drink of cold water to a man in a desert. Do not imagine that if you meet a really humble man he will be what most people call "humble" nowadays: he will not be a sort of greasy, smarmy person, who is always telling you that, of course, he is nobody.
>
> Probably all you will think about him is that he seemed a cheerful, intelligent chap who took a real interest in what you said to him.
>
> If you do dislike him it will be because you feel a little envious of anyone who seems to enjoy life so easily. He will not be thinking about humility: he will not be thinking about himself at all.[7]

People like that are difficult to offend. When we choose, ahead of time—before conversations, before meetings, before our day begins—to be unoffendable, we're simply choosing humility. And while, yes, anger happens, as we discussed earlier, it happens so much less for people whose egos are not inflamed and who have so little to lose or gain from the approval of others.

Humility means there's so much less at stake, so much less to protect.

You'll become difficult to offend simply because there's so much less of you to defend. When you are headed into a stressful social situation with difficult, offensive people, and you decide in advance, "I'm not going to let these people offend me; I'm forgiving them in advance," you are dying to yourself. You are sacrificing yourself on their behalf. You are making yourself less. You're willingly giving up your own interests and desires, because of your conviction about who Jesus is.

And Jesus tells us there's a reward for this: "Those who want to save their lives will give up true life, and those who give up their lives for me will have true life" (Matthew 16:25 NCV).

At the beginning of this book, we talked about the crazy idea that we are not entitled to anger, and how taking this idea seriously actually opens up new dimensions of rest, grace, and simplicity in our lives. We are, above all, embracing a radical humility. We're denying ourselves, doing something seemingly self-negating, and then finding that, just as Jesus promised, we haven't lost anything.

We've only gained life.

REMEMBER WHO'S DRIVING

When we lived in Houston, our kids were little, and going anywhere was a logistical nightmare. I remember, one Saturday, finally getting our kids ready to go and buckled into their seats.

We had to stop by the grocery store, so I waited in the car with the kids while Carolyn jumped out, bought her stuff, and jumped back in. We drove around some more, through another neighborhood, to drop something off at some friends'. And then we had a couple more errands to run.

We finally pulled onto I-59 south and drove for about twenty minutes in what I thought was a 65 zone. But it wasn't; it was 55. I got pulled over by a Harris County officer, and we all sat in the car until he came back with a much-deserved ticket.

Eventually we pulled off the shoulder and kept going until we turned onto another interstate. That's when my daughter took her thumb out of her mouth and said something.

"Um . . . Daddy, where are we going?"

Oh. Yeah. I should tell her.

"We're going to the big rodeo. We're going to see horses!"

"Oh! Okay."

That was it. But it dawned on me: How odd had this whole trip been, from her perspective? From the very outset, she'd just been sitting, buckled in, while we went here and there and everywhere. She'd just watched her mom run in and out, and a strange man approach the car with a funny hat and flashing lights, and we turned this way, and turned that way, and sped up and slowed down and sped up again.

And she had no idea where we were going. None. But she was cool with it.

If that were me, I'd want to know right off the bat. Where are we going? What are we doing? What's up next? Why are we doing this?

But she wasn't the least bit offended with my lack of communication. She's a child, and children are, by nature, humble. They don't have to know everything.

She knew almost nothing—not the distance, not the final destination, not the duration of our stay, not even the reason for leaving her home.

What she did know, though, mattered infinitely. It's the distinctive line between a life of mistrust, stress, exhaustion, anger, bitterness, and ceaseless striving, and a life of contentment and rest. And not just for her but for all of us who know that, ultimately, we're not in control:

She knew who was driving.

She knew, and still knows, that the one who is driving . . . loves her.

And that makes all the difference.

LOVE PEOPLE ANYWAY

SUMMING UP A BIT:

- Humans are hypocritical. They're deceptive. They tend to be obsessed with themselves. They're not as logical as they think they are. They're often blindly judgmental. They complain. And gossip too. They are—only sometimes unwittingly—cruel. They desperately want to feel good about themselves. They're prone to addiction. And so forth and on and on.
- I'm all that stuff too.
- I have to love people anyway.
- Recognizing the truth of point 2 really helps me with point 3.
- Wow, I love making lists.

I'm going to make another one soon. I think you'll like it. (I actually got excited about using bullet points for this one, but my editor said she thinks it's a bad idea. See how frustrating people can be? Sheesh.)

Given that people are aggravating, and church people are people, I can expect church people to be aggravating. (That's the transitive property of equality at work right there.) God was not naïve about this, I trust, when He decided to live among us anyway.

As an introvert with a long, even brutal list of negative church experiences, it is exceedingly easy for me to decide to try to go it alone, to avoid Christian community. But I/we simply mustn't do this.

I NEED CHRISTIAN COMMUNITY BECAUSE:

LEFT TO MYSELF, I WILL JUSTIFY ANYTHING

I need Christian community because . . . my ability to justify myself is a force of nature. It's nearly unstoppable.

We're all this way. We tend not to question our motives. We don't question our desires. We want what we want, and we will reshape reality to fit it. (I wrote extensively about this in my previous book, which you should purchase multiple copies of immediately, called *Unoffendable*.)

Left in isolation, then, we will write narratives in our heads that always feature us as the Good Person or the victim. Humans are absolute masters at this.

There's a famous Bible story of David, a "man after God's own heart" (Acts 13:22), who spots an attractive young woman. He's king, so he gets what he wants, and he has lots of women. Now he wants her. He takes her. He has her husband, a loyal soldier, sent to the front to die so he can have her to himself. He does.

He justifies it all in his head. Somehow he works it out so it's all okay. It takes a crafty, wise friend to get him to actually see how inexcusable what he's done really is.

We rewrite reality to fit what we want. It takes other people, wise people who love us, to snap us out of it.

Left to myself, I will eventually justify anything. You will too. We need honest people around us who understand this and who are willing to puncture our self-righteousness.

I NEED CHRISTIAN COMMUNITY BECAUSE:

WITHOUT IT I'M GOING TO SUFFER

I need Christian community because . . . wisdom spares me from suffering. I've learned that wisdom ultimately brings freedom, and foolishness brings pain. There are a lot of proverbs about this. Like this one:

> Spend time with the wise and you will become wise, but the friends of fools will suffer. (Proverbs 13:20 NCV)

I have to spend time with people who are humble enough to seek God's wisdom, who are growing in their understanding of the kingdom and how it actually works. I need people around me who are genuinely seeking to align themselves with what God values, rather than what the larger culture is constantly telling them to value.

My response to this in the past was simple: "Great. I need wise people. You know where I can find them? At the library. In books. I can read what they've written, and that should be enough."

Too easy.

My love of books is intense. Books are essential. They speak across generations. They challenge my thinking. They expand my horizons. Reading is fundamental, you know. Is there anything books can't do . . . ?

Why, yes, as it turns out: They can't love me.

They can't call me out, after observing life in my home, and say, "Brant, you know what? You come across too harsh with your kids."

They can't tell me they saw how I handled a tough situation and they were really proud of me. When books make me uncomfortable, I can shut them and drop them off at Goodwill. I can't really do that with humans. I've tried this.

I have to spend time with wise people—actual wise humans—and let them know me, and even let them correct me.

Once, when we were first married, my wife and I messed up our lease. We had to leave our apartment and found out our new one wasn't available for another three weeks. We were attending a church at the time, though we didn't really know anyone. They had a prayer request time at the end of the service. My wife stood up, told people about our mess-up, and said if anyone knew of somewhere we could go for a few weeks, please let us know.

A couple named Chris and Bridget told us we could stay in the guest room of their apartment. They'd been married five years, and he was finishing his PhD/MD program. They seemed nice enough. Chris was into *Lord of the Rings* and even made his own chain-mail armor, so I knew he was cool.

He was. But warning: After living with people in close community for a while, you get exposed.

One day Chris asked to sit down and talk to me. He told me, as kindly and directly as possible, that I needed to rethink how I was treating Carolyn. He said I wasn't kind enough with her. I was too stern and didn't demonstrate that I valued her. I needed to work on that, he said.

I felt dumb. It bugged me. I wanted to defend myself. But I got to see how Chris's marriage worked, too, and I respected it. I couldn't imagine how bringing this up benefited him. I knew he and Bridget actually loved us. I took it to heart.

That was a good move. It was a good three weeks.

We still thank God that we messed up our lease. I haven't talked to him for a few years, but I still think of Chris as one of my best friends ever. I'm thankful he shared his wisdom. I didn't even know I needed it.

Books can't do that. They can't kick my rear end.

I need people to spur me on. There's even a "one another" about that: "Spur one another on toward love and good deeds" (Hebrews 10:24).

The thing about spurs: They can smart a little bit. I have to be humble. I have to be willing to be lovingly corrected. If I'm not, I'm going to suffer.

I NEED CHRISTIAN COMMUNITY BECAUSE:

OTHER PEOPLE SHOW ME DIFFERENT ASPECTS OF GOD

I need Christian community because . . . other people show me different aspects of God.

I'm a big fan of "The Inklings," a group of British writers and thinkers who prodded one another artistically and spiritually in the 1930s and '40s at Oxford. C. S. Lewis, J. R. R. Tolkien, and Charles Williams were three of the principals. They certainly didn't agree on everything, but they enjoyed one another's company. Lewis, in particular, seemed to absorb the literary styles and ideas of the others. When Charles died in 1945, Lewis wrote that he'd not only miss Williams, he'd miss part of Tolkien too (here referred to as "Ronald").

> In each of my friends there is something that only some other friend can fully bring out. By myself I am not large enough to call the whole man into activity; I want other lights than my own to show all his facets. Now that Charles is dead, I shall never again see Ronald's reaction to a specifically Caroline joke. Far from having more of Ronald, having him "to myself" now that Charles is away, I have less of Ronald. Hence true Friendship is the least jealous of loves. Two friends delight to be joined by a third, and three by a fourth, if only the newcomer is qualified to become a real friend. They can then say, as the blessed souls say in Dante, "Here comes one who will augment our loves."[1]

I have to believe this dynamic is at work in our understanding of God. I might grow up with a certain perception of Him that's immature and one-sided, but it changes when I get to see, up close, how others relate to Him. I read the Bible differently. I see things through their eyes too.

I NEED CHRISTIAN COMMUNITY BECAUSE:

OTHERWISE I'M WORSHIPING ME

I need Christian community because . . . I need to confess to people.

You know how I mentioned our penchant for self-justification? And how it's *almost* unstoppable?

Confession stops it.

There are something like fifty-nine different "one anothers" in the New Testament, like the oft-repeated "love one another" (John 13:35) and "submit to one another" (Ephesians 5:21) and "offer hospitality to one another without grumbling" (1 Peter 4:9).

Another is, "Confess your sins to each other" (James 5:16).

It's so difficult and so freeing. Instead of cowering in shame, or having to jump through intellectual and moral hoops to somehow justify ourselves, we just admit we're wrong. We tell someone. We hear ourselves doing it. We are reminded of our need for humility. No more games. We expose our shame to the light of day and find that it withers.

And so often we hear those wonderful words, "Me too."

Speaking of the fifty-nine "one anothers," I need Christian community because . . . I can't do any of them myself.

Serve one another in love. Carry each other's burdens. Be patient with each other. Forgive each other. Submit to one another out of reverence for Christ. Teach one another. Encourage each other. Be kind and compassionate to one another. The list goes on and on, and none of it makes sense if I think I can do this without my spiritual brothers and sisters.

Yes, I want to avoid people or only be with a select few I find amusing, easy to be around, and who happen to affirm me and anything I want. But that requires nothing.

None of the "one anothers" make sense in that world. If I'm going to be intellectually consistent as a believer, if I have any real desire to follow Jesus, I have to obey in this area. Otherwise, I'm just worshiping me.

I NEED CHRISTIAN COMMUNITY BECAUSE:

OTHER PEOPLE NEED ME

I need Christian community because . . . other people need me.

I may be annoying and ask pesky questions, or make them wonder why I can't just go along with everything, but yes, they need me.

If I isolate myself, if I pull away from intentional community with Jesus-followers, I rob people of what I can bring to their lives. This sounds arrogant, but it's the same with everyone.

If you think you can bring nothing, you are mistaken. People often aren't aware of their own gifts or devalue them. If you put stock in Scripture, you have to accept that God has given you something to add to build up others in that context. If I isolate myself, I'm being selfish.

British theologian N. T. Wright wrote about Jesus' own vision for what "church" means:

> [Jesus] apparently envisaged that, scattered about Palestine, there would be small groups of people loyal to himself, who would get together to encourage one another, and would act as members of a family, sharing some sort of common life and, in particular, exercising mutual forgiveness.[2]

Of course, if "church" is simply an organization that offers programs and worship services, this doesn't make much sense. But if it's a family that encourages each other to spiritually grow, it's something wonderful. We all get to play.

I NEED CHRISTIAN COMMUNITY BECAUSE:

I NEED PEOPLE NOT TO BREAK UP WITH

I need Christian community because . . . I need people not to break up with. When we lived in Florida, we were part of a "simple church." We met in homes and at the beach and in restaurants.

Our group grew rapidly. There were fifty or sixty of us after a while. We got to know one another very, very well.

Once, at a Sunday gathering, a new guy invited some of the guys over for a Ping-Pong night. It was great fun.

Until it suddenly turned into a big, loud argument. It was embarrassing. I'm still not sure exactly what happened.

I remember being challenged to fight. I remember passionately making my point while gesticulating with my Ping-Pong paddle. I remember being a jerk.

I'll spare you the other details. It was one of the nastier table tennis–related evenings I've been part of.

Afterward, I wanted to leave the group—it all seemed so stupid—but I thought, *Where else do I go? These are my people.*

They're family.

There were a lot of apologies, a lot of long conversations. It took a while, but "Ping-Pong Night" became a reference we all laugh about. As ludicrous as the whole thing was, at the time, it seemed like a deal-breaker.

I was done. I wanted to move on. I know other guys did too. But we didn't. We knew we had to work it out, had to talk at length, no matter what. If churches are really just businesses, well, no problem. Move on. Make another consumer choice. But families don't just move on.

To be sure, the great thing about a church group like that is you really get to know people. The bad thing about a church group like that is you really get to know people.

People, it turns out, tend to be wrong about a lot of things. They don't raise their kids the way you raise yours. They have different standards, artistically and morally, with regard to what they'll watch on Netflix. They make bad financial decisions. What are they thinking? They're moody. They get excited about something, then don't want to follow through.

They have some theologically sketchy ideas too. Sometimes really sketchy. The whole "other people" world out there is a big mess.

A way to avoid all this, of course, is to merely attend a church service of some sort. It'll be ordered just so, and you'll see the backs of everyone's heads as they face the stage, and you can pretend everyone has their act together. It's all under control. You're in no danger whatsoever.

So here's Hansen's Law: It's only when you actually get to know people that you discover how weird everyone really is. And here's a corollary: Yep, everybody's really weird.

Still, Jesus designed us to be together. One reason, according to Wright, is that "Jesus' followers needed to know how to put into practice the way of forgiveness he was advocating."[3]

People will give you lots of occasions for practicing this, as you've probably noticed.

I wonder, too, if introverts in particular might be too perfectionistic about these relationships. We want it to be more than it can ever live up to being, so we're that much more disappointed.

Henri Nouwen wrote that there's a loneliness that will persist, even with the best of friends or church family:

> In community, where you have all the affection you could ever dream of, you feel that there is a place where even community cannot reach. That's a very important experience. In that loneliness, which is like a dark night of the soul, you learn that God is greater than community.[4]

UNITY IS A BIG DEAL TO JESUS

If unity is such a big deal to Jesus, it simply makes no sense for me to call myself His follower while remaining independent.

There's an old song about how breaking up is "hard to do," but you know what's harder than breaking up? Not breaking up.

G. K. Chesterton, who was a British writer, literary critic, and philosopher was also a champion of marriage. Even as he often waxed poetic about marriage, he knew full well how hard it could be.

> I have known many happy marriages, but never a compatible one. The whole aim of marriage is to fight through and survive the instant when incompatibility becomes unquestionable. For a man and a woman, as such, are incompatible.[5]

I think it's true beyond man/woman relationships. We're all ultimately incompatible. If I were to meet my exact clone, it would just be a matter of time before I and me would go our separate ways. We'd have some toast, quote Monty Python lines to each other, share some laughs . . . and then start getting really annoyed.

Things tend toward disorder, toward breaking down, and toward entropy and decay. Our refusal to break up, our refusal to isolate out of a desire for convenience or fear of being hurt, is evidence of life.

It's also evidence that grace is real, and it works.

Yes, Jesus-followers are an odd group. Some are hard to take. Some are annoying. Some would say the same of me. But there's something wonderful, mysterious, even shocking, about people who stay together anyway.

The Limo Is Coming for You Anyway

My son is like me. He's not much into athletics. But we signed him up for a flag-football league when he was in sixth grade. My wife told me the league needed someone to coach my son's team, the Rams, and I told her, point-blank, I would not be doing it. I know nothing about coaching football. Nothing. "I will not be coaching the Rams," I said.

The park district called me before the first practice and told me about the Rams, and how they needed a coach, and would I do it? I told them no. "I'm sorry; I just can't do that; it's out of the question. I will not be coaching the Rams."

I dropped Justice off at practice, and all the teams went to different parts of the practice fields. They all had coaches. The Rams assembled, and everyone's parents had dropped them off, and I towered over all the kids. They asked me if I was their coach. I told them no. "I'm sorry, I will play catch right now, but I will not be coaching the Rams."

The smallest kid, a little scraggly-blond kid named Jared, threw the ball back and forth with me. He asked me again if I would coach. I told him, again, no. They'd have to find someone else to coach the Rams.

He caught the ball, stopped, and looked at me. He said, "Okay, but can I please at least call you 'Coach'? I've always wanted to call someone 'Coach.'"

When I got home, I had to tell my wife why I was carrying a big bag of footballs, pylons, and flags. I was now coaching the Rams.

I was clueless. Over the first eight games, we not only didn't win, *we didn't score any points.* My offensive coordination was truly, you know, offensive. During practices, we'd all look over at the Yellow Shirt Team Over There, the team that had six football coaching dads, fancy drills, and all the football-y . . . things. They were amazing, a well-oiled machine.

I think we were still trying to get our practice ball inflated.

I think we hit rock bottom when we were penalized for wearing illegal shorts. (Apparently, you can't wear shorts with pockets in flag football.) To avoid forfeiture, I sent my team into the crowd of parents to randomly ask people if they could swap shorts with them. Yes, that's always a low point, the borrowing-shorts-from-the-crowd point of the football season.

And we played that team, the Yellow Shirt Team Over There, the one with the dads with visors and whistles and multiple future NCAA recruits, the very last game of the season.

We were 0–11. They were 11–0. Sounds like we had no chance, right? Sounds like there's no way in the world we could possibly beat these guys, right?

Something incredible happened. Our best player, a little guy named Christian, returned the opening kickoff for a touchdown. We were ahead 6–0!

So the team that supposedly "didn't have a chance;" who had the "worst" and "most clueless" coach in the league? *We now led the game over the mighty Yellow Team!* There were gasps from the crowd. Could the impossible happen? Do you believe in miracles?

I patrolled the sidelines, and confidently called the next play. My hopes soared. *This could become one of those Christian movies!*

And then they scored 77 unanswered points. We lost 77–6.

So, yeah, it's not really that great of a story.

Except for one thing. As our dejected, winless kids left the field, the kids who went 0–12 and just got humiliated again, something wonderful happened, something you usually don't see in football.

A white stretch limousine pulled up along the field, a limo with flags. Rams flags.

Everyone stopped and stared: the Rams, the playoff-bound Yellow Team, everybody. And a mom said, "Guys, it's time for your end-of-season party!"

The Rams went from dejected losers to royalty. Just like that. They were smiling and laughing and jumping up and down. They all piled into the limo, and off they went for our big pizza-and-swim party.

The Yellow Team, coaches and all, were in awe.

This is how the kingdom of God works. The last are first, the first are last, and in the end, as much as we want to think our performance is all that matters, ultimately, the victory has exactly nothing to do with us.

In the end, you're free to flail and fumble all you want, kids, because here's a sweet thought:

The limo is coming for you anyway.

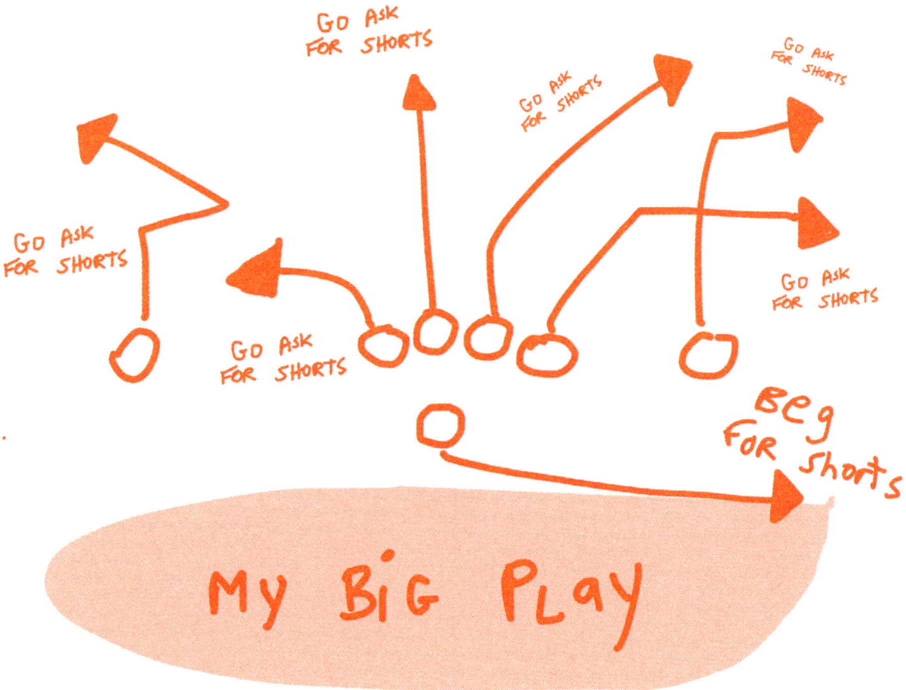

GOD IS MY DEFENDER

So let's review: Choosing to be unoffendable means choosing to be humble. Not only that, the practice teaches humility. Once you've decided you can't control other people; once you've reconciled yourself to the fact that the world, and its people, are broken; once you've realized your own moral failure before God; once you've abandoned the idea that your significance comes from anything other than God, you're growing in humility, and that's exactly where God wants us all.

It's contrary to seemingly everything in our culture, but the more we divest ourselves of ourselves, the better our lives get. Jesus told us as much. He said if we'd give up our lives, for His sake, we'd find real life.

When we surrender our perceived "rights," when we let go of our attempts to manipulate, we find—surprise!—joy.

I've seen it happen in my own life, in little bits. I'm still learning. But I'm so glad someone told me to choose to be unoffendable, because something clicked in my understanding of what it means to follow Jesus. It turns out that life is not only more joy-filled for me but more attractive to others.

I have to die to myself. What I'm finding is it doesn't happen all at once, and it's simultaneously simple to understand and arduous to actually do. But little by little, I think I'm seeing what God is up to.

He wants to be in control. And you know what? I want Him to be. This hasn't always been the case. I think I can trust Him. I don't need to control things anymore. There's so much less at stake when I let go, so much less of me to defend, so much less of "my way" to get in the way and feed my anger.

What a relief. God tells us to die to ourselves, and get rid of anger, for a reason: He loves us.

And I guess I always knew that, that He loves us. But I'm now less prone to anger, and more prone to forgive, because I'm finally really believing, a bit more, day by day, that He actually loves me.

Why am I so stressed? Why do I need to pretend I can control people? Why do I need to make myself "significant"? Why do I think I need to assess other people spiritually? Why am I always trying to assess myself spiritually? Why do I need to defend myself?

God is my Defender. He's in control. And no, I don't know where I'm going, but I know He loves me.

I KNOW HOW IT ALL ENDS

"We've just got to watch this game. It's HUGE," I told my family. "So, so huge."

They knew I was telling the truth, because I never said stuff like this. We didn't even treat the Super Bowl this way. It was the NCAA Tournament, and the winner of this game would go to the Final Four. My alma mater, the University of Illinois, was playing Arizona. We were favored to win the national championship for the first time in my life. We only had one loss that whole season so far, and it was a buzzer-beating fluke.

We sat down to watch, my wife, Carolyn, my son, Justice, and me. I was so pumped . . . until we stunk. We did nothing right. Our shot selection was terrible. The refs were awful. The coaching decisions were ridiculous. Our players suddenly forgot how to run and dribble. The announcers were biased. Even the crowd was annoying.

I was ticked. I was anxious. I was unnerved. I was also obnoxious.

"That's it. Just shut it off," I said, getting up to leave. I mean, we were down 15 points with just a few minutes left. It was over. But my wife was not cool with this attitude.

"Brant, stop it. Your son just wants to watch a game with you."

"Okay, great. Let's watch 'em lose!" I said, behaving not unlike, say, a big baby. And then the most epic comeback in NCAA history began. Illinois won in overtime.

Amazing. Breathtaking. I've re-watched that game about 42,000 times on YouTube, and I get goosebumps every time.

And you know what's interesting? When I'm re-watching the game, for some reason, I'm not consumed with anger. I'm not mad at the announcers and the refs and the team and the crowd. My body is not filled with cortisol. My blood pressure does not go up. I'm not anxious in the least. I'm at peace. I just enjoy it.

Why? I mean, it's the same game, right? Why am I at peace?

What explains this?

Simple: I know how it all ends.

That, my friend, is everything.

NOTES

1–10

1. Look it up on YouTube: When the gates swing open, the cows dance with glee, and now I realize I totally should have had a photo of that on the cover of this book, and maybe changed the title: *Life Is Hard. God Is Good. Check Out These Awesome Cows.*

2. Don Roy King, "Unfrozen Caveman Lawyer," transcript, SNL Transcripts, October 8, 2018, https://snltranscripts.jt.org/91/91gcaveman.phtml.

3. Brian Kolodiejchuk, *Mother Teresa: Come Be My Light: The Private Writings of the Saint of Calcutta* (Doubleday, 2009), 288.

4. Christopher Hitchens, quoted in David Van Biema, "Mother Teresa's Crisis of Faith," *Time*, August 23, 2007, https://time.com/4126238/mother-teresas-crisis-of-faith/.

5. Frank Viola, "Living Without Offense," *Beyond Evangelical* (blog), October 12, 2009, https://www.frankviola.org/2009/10/12/living-without-offense-rick-warren-is-supporting-our-twitter-conference-tomorrow/.

11–20

1. Joni Eareckson Tada, *Anger: Aim It in the Right Direction* (Rose Publishing, 2012), 12.

2. Svetlana Alliluyeva, *Only One Year: How Joseph Stalin's Daughter Broke Through the Iron Curtain, a Memoir* (HarperCollins, 2024).

3. Brant Hansen, "New Worship Song—Break Their Teeth (Inspired by Psalm 3)," YouTube, 2 min., 37 sec., https://www.youtube.com/watch?v=XyidEorRDMc.

4. Tammy Lenski, "Venting Anger: A Good Habit to Break," Mediate, May 2011, https://hr.uci.edu/partnership/mediation/pdf/Venting-Anger.pdf; Denis Storey, "It Might Be Time to Rethink How We Handle Anger," April 3, 2024, https://www.psychiatrist.com/news/it-might-be-time-to-rethink-how-we-handle-anger/#:~:text=Clinical%20relevance:%20New%20research%20challenges,Anger%20Analysis.
5. Gail Cornwall and Juli Fraga, "Stop Venting! It Doesn't Work," *Slate*, March 8, 2022, https://slate.com/technology/2022/03/venting-makes-you-feel-worse-psychology-research.html.
6. Rob Bricken, "7 Moments in the Bible When Jesus Acted Very Un-Jesus-Like," Gizmodo, September 16, 2015, https://gizmodo.com/7-moments-in-the-bible-when-jesus-acted-very-un-jesus-l-1731054203.
7. Thomas Merton, *Thoughts in Solitude* (Farrar, Straus and Giroux, 1999), 79.
8. Dallas Willard, *The Allure of Gentleness: Defending the Faith in the Manner of Jesus* (HarperOne, 2015), 31.
9. Brennan Manning, *The Signature of Jesus* (Multnomah, 1996), 44–45.
10. C. S. Lewis, *Mere Christianity*, rev. and amp. ed. (HarperSanFrancisco, 2009), 93.
11. Ryann Blackshere, "Widower Forges Friendship with Man in Crash That Killed Wife, Unborn Baby," *Today*, February 3, 2014, NBC News, https://www.today.com/news/man-crash-killed-woman-forges-friendship-her-widower-2D12044681.
12. Iain McGilchrist, *The Matter with Things: Our Brains, Our Delusions, and the Unmaking of the World*, 2 vols. (Perspectiva, 2021), vol. 1, 464, quoting E. B. Ford (italics added by the author).

21–30

1. "Neighbors Remember Serial Killer as Serial Killer," *The Onion*, April 22, 1998, https://theonion.com/neighbors-remember-serial-killer-as-serial-killer-1819564698/.

2. Jon Ward, "This Is What Happens When Hip-Hop Lets the Saints In," *Huffington Post*, February 21, 2014, https://www.huffpost.com/entry/lecrae-moore-rap-christian_n_4784064.

3. Mike Yaconelli, *Messy Spirituality* (Zondervan, 2002), 54.

4. Yaconelli, *Messy Spirituality*, 126–27.

31–40

1. Robert M. Sapolsky, *Why Zebras Don't Get Ulcers* (W. H. Freeman, 1994).

2. "Gratitude in the Bible: Give Thanks with a Grateful Heart," Tithely, September 10, 2024, https://get.tithe.ly/blog/gratitude-in-the-bible-give-thanks-with-a-grateful-heart.

3. Douglas Webster, *The Easy Yoke* (NavPress, 1995), 163–64.

41–50

1. University of British Columbia, "Slacktivism: 'Liking' on Facebook May Mean Less Giving," ScienceDaily, November 8, 2013, https://www.sciencedaily.com/releases/2013/11/131108091320.htm.

2. Arthur C. Brooks, *Who Really Cares* (Basic Books, 2007).

3. Christopher A. Hall, "The Gift of Anger," *Christianity Today*, January 1, 2004, https://www.christianitytoday.com/2004/01/gift-of-anger/.

4. Gregory L. Janz and Ann McMurray, "When Is It OK to Be Angry?," (book excerpt), CBN, http://www.cbn.com/entertainment/books/jantz-guide-to-managing-anger.aspx.
5. Dallas Willard, "Divine Conspiracy 11: Living Without Anger," 1:20:59, lecture recorded during the Harvey Fellows 2007 Summer Institute, posted by "Daniel Vieira" June 22, 2011, https://www.youtube.com/watch?v=NBBB9G6WW3w.
6. James Bryan Smith, *The Good and Beautiful Life: Putting on the Character of Christ* (InterVarsity Press, 2009), 179.

51–60

1. Betty Gold et al., "22 Easy 4th of July Menu Ideas for the Ultimate Backyard Barbecue," *Real Simple*, April 26, 2025, https://www.realsimple.com/food-recipes/recipe-collections-favorites/seasonal/4th-of-july-menu-ideas.
2. Dan Snow, "Dan Snow Explains the Epic Battle of Hastings," September 25, 2025, posted by Dan Snow's History Hit, YouTube, 1:01:34, https://www.youtube.com/watch?v=BI7nPfCk84I.
3. Dallas Willard, *Hearing God: Developing a Conversational Relationship with God* (InterVarsity Press, 2012), 243.
4. Brennan Manning, *The Ragamuffin Gospel: Good News for the Bedraggled, Beat-Up, and Burnt Out* (Multnomah Books, 1990), 29.
5. Charles Wesley, "And Can It Be That I Should Gain," 1739.
6. "With Groupon, Fun Never Ends," Groupon, accessed November 12, 2025, https://www.groupon.com/landing/fun-never-ends?srsltid=AfmBOooYpBu-yLhpw8KAfexOqKRhau3AeWBpJw5LblQLBFYjk-ErNDH7.

61–70

1. Khaled Hosseini, *And the Mountains Echoed* (Riverhead, 2013), Kindle, loc. 1435–37.

2. Tony Campolo, *The Kingdom of God Is a Party: God's Radical Plan for His Family* (Thomas Nelson, 1990), 5–6.

3. Campolo, *The Kingdom of God Is a Party*, 8.

4. Henri Nouwen, *Gracias: A Latin American Journal*, repr. (Orbis, 1993), 147–48.

5. Timothy Keller, "Peace—Overcoming Anxiety" (sermon), *Timothy Keller Podcast*, April 10, 2013, https://podcast.gospelinlife.com/e/peace---overcoming-anxiety/.

6. Lance Ford, *Unleader* (Beacon Hill, 2013), 26.

7. C. S. Lewis, *Mere Christianity* (Touchstone, 1996), 121.

71–80

1. C. S. Lewis, *The Four Loves* (Harcourt Brace, 1960), 61.

2. N. T. Wright, *Jesus and the Victory of God* (SPCK Publishing, 1996), 297.

3. Wright, *Jesus and the Victory of God*, 296.

4. Henri Nouwen, interviewed by Darryl Tippens, "Loneliness and Community: An Interview with Henri Nouwen," *Wineskins* 2, no. 7 (March–August 1994): 14–19.

5. G. K. Chesterton, *What's Wrong with the World* (Dodd, Mead and Company, 1912), 67–68.

DISCOVER MORE FROM
BRANT HANSEN

Available Wherever Books Are Sold

Don't Tune Out...Tune in!

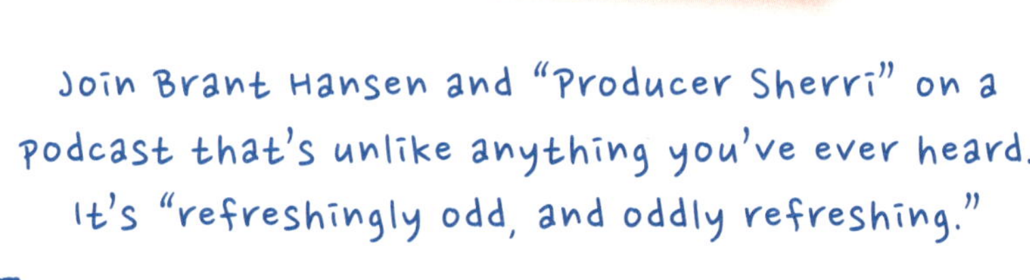

Join Brant Hansen and "Producer Sherri" on a podcast that's unlike anything you've ever heard. It's "refreshingly odd, and oddly refreshing."

It's funny, authentic, and spiritually encouraging. More than 20 million downloads so far!

Available on any major podcast platform.

THE LIVING UNOFFENDED PODCAST

WITH BRANT HANSEN

Let's keep talking about this! Join Brant each week for discussion and encouragement about forgiveness, loving our neighbors and enemies, and following Jesus. Available on: